T0369698

10 PRINCIPLES
for Doing Effective Couples Therapy

The Norton Series on Interpersonal Neurobiology
Louis Cozolino, PhD, Series Editor
Allan N. Schore, PhD, Series Editor, 2007–2014

Daniel J. Siegel, MD, Founding Editor

The field of mental health is in a tremendously exciting period of growth and conceptual reorganization. Independent findings from a variety of scientific endeavors are converging in an interdisciplinary view of the mind and mental well-being. An interpersonal neurobiology of human development enables us to understand that the structure and function of the mind and brain are shaped by experiences, especially those involving emotional relationships.

The Norton Series on Interpersonal Neurobiology provides cutting-edge, multidisciplinary views that further our understanding of the complex neurobiology of the human mind. By drawing on a wide range of traditionally independent fields of research—such as neurobiology, genetics, memory, attachment, complex systems, anthropology, and evolutionary psychology—these texts offer mental health professionals a review and synthesis of scientific findings often inaccessible to clinicians. The books advance our understanding of human experience by finding the unity of knowledge, or consilience, that emerges with the translation of findings from numerous domains of study into a common language and conceptual framework. The series integrates the best of modern science with the healing art of psychotherapy.

A Norton Professional Book

10 PRINCIPLES
for Doing Effective Couples Therapy

Julie Schwartz Gottman, PhD

AND

John M. Gottman, PhD

FOREWORD BY

Daniel J. Siegel

W. W. NORTON & COMPANY
NEW YORK LONDON

Note to Readers: Standards of clinical practice and protocol change over time, and no technique or recommendation is guaranteed to be safe or effective in all circumstances. This volume is intended as a general information resource for professionals practicing in the field of psychotherapy and mental health; it is not a substitute for appropriate training, peer review, and/or clinical supervision. Neither the publisher nor the author(s) can guarantee the complete accuracy, efficacy, or appropriateness of any particular recommendation in every respect.

Printed in the United States of America
First Edition

For information about permission to reproduce selections from this book,
write to Permissions, W. W. Norton & Company, Inc.,
500 Fifth Avenue, New York, NY 10110

For information about special discounts for bulk purchases, please contact
W. W. Norton Special Sales at specialsales@wwnorton.com or 800-233-4830

Manufacturing by Sheridan Books
Book design by Carole Desnoes
Production manager: Christine Critelli

Library of Congress Cataloging-in-Publication Data
Gottman, Julie Schwartz.
10 principles for doing effective couples therapy / Julie Schwartz
Gottman, John M. Gottman. — First edition.
pages cm. — (A Norton professional book)
Includes bibliographical references and index.
ISBN 978-0-393-70835-6 (hardcover)
1. Couples therapy. 2. Counseling. 3. Therapist and patient.
I. Gottman, John Mordechai. II. Title. III. Title: Ten principles
for doing effective couples therapy.
RC488.5.G678 2015
616.89'1562 — dc23
2015024253

W. W. Norton & Company, Inc.
500 Fifth Avenue, New York, N.Y. 10110
www.wwnorton.com

W. W. Norton & Company Ltd.
15 Carlisle Street, London W1D 3BS

0

To Etana Kunovsky
who brought the
Gottman Institute to life.

Contents

Foreword

By Daniel J. Siegel

When we work as mental health professionals, we are in a wonderful and challenging position to focus fully on what both "mental" and "health" really mean, and on how to cultivate optimal well-being in others' lives. With so many distinct fields contributing to this broad profession, it ought not be surprising to find that we have so many different approaches. For a young trainee or even a seasoned practitioner in the art of psychotherapy, such diversity in what comprises the field can be overwhelming, and even outright confusing. Where do you turn for sage advice? What is the basic framework from which you choose your interventions? How do you formulate your understanding of the nature of a client or patient's challenges? How do you plan a treatment strategy, implement it appropriately, and assess its outcome?

For over two decades, several colleagues and I have been eager to find a common, scientifically-grounded framework for the broad field of mental health. Whatever our field of origin, from psychology and psychiatry to social work and psychiatric nursing, from educational and occupational therapy to music and dance therapy, we have the opportunity to come together to address some interrelated and fundamental questions: What is the mind? What is a healthy mind and how do we cultivate it? What can we do as mental health professionals to keep up-to-date on cutting-edge science and therapeutic approaches that inform how we approach, plan, and implement psychotherapy? Can we have a common framework that unites the field of caring for the mind that is based on weaving science with wise clinical practice?

To address these questions, the field of Interpersonal Neurobiology (IPNB) was created at the end of the last millennium. We use what E.O. Wilson (1998) would call a "consilient" approach, in which we seek out the foundational findings of distinct disciplines—ones that do not often communicate directly with each other—and identify common themes that emerge from their independent pursuits of knowledge. These "universal" discoveries have special meaning for understanding reality, and for our field of mental health in that they give us unique insights into understanding the nature of life and being human. IPNB is not a form of therapy; it informs therapy. The conceptual framework that emerges from trying to understand the consilient view of the nature of our lives can be used in a range of fields, including education, child-rearing, and psychotherapy. IPNB attempts to "bring science to life" as it finds the consilient foundations, builds a broad interdisciplinary framework that links science and clinical work, and then applies this view to helping people live with more well-being.

10 Principles for Doing Effective Couples Therapy is a wonderful example of how to combine a range of scientific ideas and research findings and apply them for everyday use in the practice of psychotherapy. This is science-based clinical work at its best. This practical and insightful compendium by leaders in the field of relational science and its clinical application offers direct guidance on how to inform your own clinical practice. Julie Schwartz Gottman, PhD, and John M. Gottman, PhD, have been studying romantic relationships and the implementation and assessment of couples therapy for decades. And here in your hands you hold the wisdom and practical pearls of these two masters of relational health.

In this brief foreword, I will identify some initial ways in which each of these 10 principles illuminates the foundations of IPNB. Julie, John, and I have taught together, and weaving their magnificent contributions to our understanding of interpersonal connections—when they go well and when they fall apart—with the consilient principles of IPNB has been a fascinating, fun, and fruitful collaboration. I am honored to have their life's work as an important part of our Norton Professional Library on IPNB that we all hope will serve as a foundational scientific core framework for the field of mental health.

The First Principle: Use Research-Based Methods to Treat Couples. While it is true that not everything that is meaningful can be measured, and not everything that can be measured is meaningful, in our field of mental health it is important to begin with a clearly thought-out, scientifically-grounded approach to the challenges we are trying to address in our work. One person in treatment is challenging enough; with two in the room with us, the complexity is both increased and made more visible.

In IPNB we say that our approach to mental health needs to be consistent with science but not constrained by it. What this means is that we draw on science as a starting place, but acknowledge that as specialists of the mind, and the mind being the source of subjective experience, we can never fully measure this core mental feature. Yet as visionary leaders in relational science, the Gottmans have beautifully shown that when couples do not focus on the internal subjective experience of each member of the pair, the health of the relationship suffers. As you read about their research findings, you may find support for what you may have felt intuitively: Healthy relationships require that we honor and support one another's differentiated experiences. In many ways, this scientific finding is consistent with one major principle of IPNB: Health emerges from integration. Integration is the differentiation and linkage of different elements in a system. Integration in a relationship entails the honoring of differences and the compassionate communication that links two individuals together as a whole. Integration is the source of the notion that "the whole is greater than the sum of its parts" and this is exactly what the Gottmans' research findings reveal.

The Second Principle: Assess First, Then Decide on Treatment. In IPNB we discuss the profound importance of seeing the mind as an emergent, self-organizing, embodied, and relational process that regulates the flow of energy and information. Your own mind as a clinician becomes a part of the emergent process within therapy. If we do not identify our prior expectations and judgments before we begin treatment—what can be called our "top-down" ideas—we may be vulnerable to not being fully present for our clients or patients. Instead of sensing what they really need, we may impose what we were thinking before they even entered the room.

The second principle reminds us to keep an open mind, use our skills to evaluate the full nature of what is going on, and then make a deliberate choice to decide on a treatment strategy. From an IPNB perspective, this is how we differentiate each person, each couple, each family: we see and then link ourselves to them in the therapeutic relationship to create an integrated approach to psychotherapy. We as clinicians are a part of a larger process. Keeping our own minds open and differentiating assessment from treatment planning and implementation enables us to proactively create a more effective and integrated approach to our work.

The Third Principle: Understand Each Partner's Inner World. "Standing under" each person in treatment means sensing their subjective inner experience, making sense of this world, and honoring the validity of this felt texture of lived life. We have at least two streams of perception: One is of the physical world, the events we can see with our eyes or hear with our ears, for example. The other is the mental world, the subjective experience of our feelings, thoughts, hopes, and dreams. Too often in school, and sadly too commonly in our home life, we tend to focus primarily on physical sight, the perception of the world of objects. In contrast, we have "mindsight," the ability to sense the subjective mental lives of others, and of ourselves.

This third principle highlights the IPNB notion that mindsight is at the heart of healthy relationships and of effective psychotherapy. Mindsight is a teachable skill; when we model mindsight with our own behavior as therapists, we can inspire couples to learn to sense and respect each other's inner world. Mindsight is comprised of three parts: Insight, Empathy, and Integration. When we teach mindsight to others through our example as well as through direct instruction, we are building the skills of self-understanding, other-understanding, and the core process of integration at the heart of kindness and compassion.

The Fourth Principle: Map Your Treatment Route. Although some physicists are now writing that time may not exist, things in life do change in space. So change is real. And when we have a sense of a direction—what is called "intention"—we can actually map out where we are going, as we do when we set a course while sailing. We set a course, but need to be flexible in how we move toward our general goal.

In IPNB we view "mental time travel" as the important way we make sense of life, connecting the past, being open in the present, and taking an active part in charting out the future. This principle resonates with us as professionals, as we build on our knowledge of the past in both our scientifically-grounded framework and our awareness of the couples' history, strive to be open and present in the moment, and then actively map out the intentional but flexible direction for treatment.

The Fifth Principle: Soothe Yourself, Then Intervene. The Gottmans have powerfully woven their work with that of other IPNB authors, particularly Steve Porges (2011) and Jaak Panksepp (Panksepp and Biven, 2012). In exploring these authors' powerful findings and framework, they reveal the importance of our own emotional state, and how we need to be in an open, receptive mindset to engage effectively in psychotherapy. When clients or patients "push our own buttons" we can enter a reactive state, turning on the brainstem's fight-flight-freeze-or-faint reaction to threat, and lose our ability to think clearly and flexibly. This is how we enter survival mode.

In IPNB we see integration as health that arises naturally from a receptive state. In Porges' terms (2011), we move from reactivity to receptivity as we turn on a social engagement system. This principle reminds us that it is from this open, receptive state that healing happens. We see that such presence is the portal from which integration naturally arises. When you model for your couples how to keep yourself in that state of receptive presence, you are teaching them skills for doing it themselves and for each other.

The Sixth Principle: Process Past Regrettable Incidents. In the IPNB foundations, we see that there are several domains of integration. These include the integration of consciousness, bilateral integration, vertical integration, memory integration, narrative integration, state integration, interpersonal integration, temporal integration, and identity integration. This sixth principle draws on several of these interconnected domains, especially that of memory integration. In the brain, an experience is encoded into implicit and explicit layers of memory. After encoding, a changed neural firing pattern is stored in the brain and has the potential of later firing in a pattern similar, but not identical to, that which was initially there at encoding. Retrieval of memory is the activation of that similar pattern, stored after encoding, which actively influences our lives and consciousness through feelings, thoughts, images, and behavior.

When a "regrettable incident" has been encoded and stored in memory, it can be both at an implicit and explicit level, and it can alter how we feel about another person in ways that persist for long periods of time following the experience. From an attachment research perspective, this can often be seen as a rupture in a relationship. Such a rupture embeds itself in memory in such a way as to impair memory integration and leave retrieval prone to chaos or rigidity. Without honoring the research-proven importance of repairing the rupture, this incident can seriously diminish the vitality of a relationship. From an IPNB perspective, such ruptures are examples of a state of compromised integration, a state prone to chaos or rigidity or both. Repair takes the impaired differentiation and/or linkage of this non-integrated experience in memory and in the relationship and directly enhances the honoring of differences and the cultivation of compassionate linkages. This is how repair is an integrative act, both within us and between us. The research of the Gottmans looks at the crucial importance of "processing" this rupture, this regrettable incident. From an IPNB viewpoint, this processing integrates the non-integrated incident in both the memory system and the relational system, catalyzing both internal and interpersonal integration.

The Seventh Principle: Replace the Four Horsemen with Gentle Conflict Management Skills. Of the many insights the Gottmans' research has revealed, a foundational one is that challenged couples experience four elements of dysfunction in the ways they relate to each other: 1) criticism; 2) contempt; 3) defensiveness; and, 4) stonewalling. As the Gottmans reveal, the first two are used as active weapons against each other; the second two are used as isolating and protective shields. From an IPNB perspective, these four elements are examples of impaired relational integration. Criticism and contempt reveal the chaotic bank outside the river of integration; defensiveness and stonewalling are the bank of rigidity. Each blocks differentiation and linkage.

With integration emerges harmony. And so the Four Horsemen are direct relational assaults on the harmony of a "masters" approach to effective relationality, and instead reveal the perpetuating blockages of integration present with the "disasters" of relationships. The Gottmans' research clearly demonstrates that replacing these Horsemen with gentle approaches to managing communication is an effective and necessary strategy. In IPNB terms, we see this move as the core of therapeutic work to cultivate integration to bring more harmony and vitality to a couple.

The Eighth Principle: Strengthen Friendship and Intimacy. There are so many ways we connect in a close relationship as a couple. IPNB views these connections as inherently honoring differences and promoting compassionate communication in linking together to cultivate an integrated relationship. Strengthening these ways of integrating is how IPNB views the Gottmans' suggestion about friendship and intimacy. If you think about friendship, you may be able to notice how close friendships require that you honor differences and promote respectful, caring communication. Each person is unique, and each person can be connected to the other without losing his or her own identity.

During sexual intimacy, the importance of differentiation and of linkage in a romantic relationship is also highlighted. As Robert Stoller, MD, would state in his various writings as well as to me as his student, in his studies of sexuality he found that we are both deeply focused on our own internal experience and yet also connected so openly to another's. This is the way we differentiate and link in optimal sexual joining experiences. Strengthening friendship and intimacy deeply cultivates integration in our relationships.

The Ninth Principle: Suspend Moral Judgment When Treating Affairs. Being mindfully aware entails letting go of our propensity to filter ongoing perceptions through the lens of previously existing judgments, or "prejudgments", and attempting to be open to whatever arises as it arises. COAL is an IPNB acronym for being curious, open, accepting, and loving, and is one way of describing this experience of presence within mindful awareness. When an affair is a part of a couple's history, your own mindful awareness and COAL state will be crucial in helping the two individuals find a way to repair this rupture in their integrated relationship. Through the many clinical case reports and descriptions of the internal experience of the clinician offered in this book, you will find inspiring suggestions for how to apply each of these principles in your own work. Our presence as a therapist is a key facilitator for guiding a couple to find the courage and commitment to try to repair the rupture of an affair, to reestablish integration, or at times even to create integration anew.

This principle reminds us that we, too, are a part of the healing process. Healing is becoming whole. Such wholeness, from IPNB's consilient viewpoint, emerges as a self-organizing process that has a natural drive to create harmony, a flexible and adaptive state that is created with integration. In many ways, then, we must work to create that state of presence that is a portal for integration to naturally arise in the complex system of the couple. An affair reveals an impediment to that integration, and our own moral judgments about the affair can contribute to furthering that blockage. Empowering each member of the couple to explore in a differentiated way what went on to make an affair arise—with thoughtful limitations carefully identified in this book—can make repair possible and facilitate the integrative process of healing, of making whole again.

The Tenth Principle: Dive Deep to Create Shared Meaning. The domains of integration of narrative, state, memory, consciousness, temporality, and identity each come to mind as relevant to this important last principle. Meaning emerges from our lives within our shared narratives that are woven into the tapestry of our personal identity, as well as our collective identity as a couple. Meaning comes from deep inquiries into what matters in life. When we explore this inner mindscape, we are using our mindsight skills to develop insight into ourselves. When we share this with our partner, we are harnessing mindsight's empathic skill. And when we dive deep to explore and co-create our unfolding meaning, we are cultivating mindsight's integration, that compassionate and kind stance toward ourselves and toward others.

In implementing all of the principles you'll explore in this magnificent book, you may find that your own life's integration becomes enhanced. Finding meaning in serving the well-being of others is one of the secret treasures of being a mental health professional. With Julie and John Gottman's important visions for using science to understand and improve our relational health, we are given the wonderful opportunity to help each other find this meaning, share our lives, and bring more kindness and compassion into this world. What more can we ask for? Enjoy!

—Daniel J. Siegel, MD
Founding Series Editor,
Norton Series on Interpersonal Neurobiology

Preface

We love doing couples therapy. For decades we've hoped our colleagues would feel likewise and choose to pursue the same specialty. It's true that the proliferation of family therapy training programs has led to a flood of counselors working with families. Yet we still see therapists giving a wide berth to couples work.

During the 17 years John worked at the University of Washington, he gave an annual lecture to psychology interns. Whenever he asked them what training in couples therapy they had received, they always replied, "You're it." Only a few had treated a couple during their internship, and many said they ran away from couples' therapy like hikers from a six-foot grizzly bear. Apparently couples therapy wasn't a specialty high on their list.

Yet wherever our work takes us, we hear the same story: Couples everywhere are drowning. In far-flung countries like Turkey, Japan, Sweden, and Mexico, marriages are steeped in loneliness. Partners reach out for connection bearing axes in their hands. They want to be held but clothe themselves with spikes. They want to be known but wear masks impenetrable like armor. Intimacy is impossible. No wonder they suffer.

William Doherty's studies at the University of Minnesota revealed that the number one problem people raise in individual therapy is a love relationship issue. But like some kind of cruel joke, researcher Alan Gurman found that therapy clients discussing a relationship issue in individual therapy is a great predictor of divorce. Gurman noted that individual therapists hear only half the story. As therapy progresses, they buy the tales of that wretched "Other," sympathize with their beleaguered clients, and push them to dump the nasty troll under a bridge and run for their lives. Rarely if ever do they actually meet the troll. This is not a great formula for building lasting relationships or furthering clients' well-being for that matter.

Millions of people around the world are clamoring for help with their relationships, and for good reason. Divorce rates are rising on nearly every continent. So are the suicide rates of children. It's no surprise, given the unhappiness that saturates their family homes.

Thousands of studies show that the quality of parenting determines the future trajectory of children's lives. We also know that the quality of parenting is directly correlated with the quality of the marriage. Better marriages predict better outcomes for the children. In his lab, John found that the amount of stress hormones that show up in a child's 24-hour urine sample accurately reflects the quality of the parents' relationship. The worse the marriage, the more stress hormones there are in the child's urine. There's no question that the cradle that holds the child is the parental relationship. That cradle can either gently soothe the child to sleep or violently throw her to the floor.

Hardier souls like U.S. soldiers may be trained to gun down the enemy, yet when it comes to love relationships, they are as tender as the rest of us. Studies conducted by army researchers show that 58 percent of the time that a soldier attempts suicide (and too often succeeds), the attempt is preceded by a fight between the soldier and his or her Stateside partner on cell phone or Skype. Unfortunately, angry words can sometimes be more devastating than bullets.

There is also no question that love relationships affect our physical health as well as our emotional well-being. Many studies have repeatedly shown that a higher quality relationship predicts not only better health but also stronger recovery from illness and a longer life span.

The message is clear: If we therapists want to help our clients, it's crucial that we learn how to help our clients' ailing relationships.

In our years of training therapists to do couples therapy, we often hear how scary the work is. It certainly can be. Nobody wants to face two dragons trying to immolate each other. We even feel scared sometimes, and we've been doing this work for decades. Though challenging, however, couples therapy is some of the most gratifying work we've had the privilege to do. We think it can be like that for you, too.

When you see a couple, you have two people in front of you, each with very different internal experiences and sometimes opposing goals for coming to you. You know you need to treat the relationship, but how are you supposed to pin down something as elusive as a relationship, let alone, change it? Compared with an individual client, a relationship is an entirely different animal. What should you do first? What should you look for? What questions should you ask? If they give different answers, whom should you believe? Which one is right if they argue in front of you? Which one is the culprit, and which one is innocent? Whom should you empathize with? How do you empathize with both partners if they have opposite points of view? And if they end up separating later on, does that mean you failed? Are you only successful if you keep them together? Then there's all that emotion and personal history they may stir up in you. What do you do with that?

You probably ask questions like these, because we've asked them ourselves for decades and still do. These are the questions we want to address.

Let's begin a journey from the safe comfort of your armchair. We'll share our stories with you, both successes and failures. Our couples have taught us everything we know, which we have refined into our top 10 principles for doing effective couples therapy.

We introduce the subject of couples therapy from the very beginning: What it's like to start with a new couple with all of their tortured anxieties and our own. Then we describe the lessons we've learned from watching 3,000 couples over the course of nearly four decades of research. Next we translate our research findings into methods for assessing a couple, including each individual partner and their relationship, and from there how to plan their treatment.

The following chapters provide the foundations for doing effective couples intervention. We discuss how to soothe yourself when a couple is battling in front of you so you can hang in there and help, rather than excusing yourself and dashing out the back door (we've all been there); how to encourage couples at war to shelve their rocket launchers and unearth their empathy instead; how to help couples who have dwelled for years in separate wings of their home to reunite; how to adjust your own moral compass when treating the clients who have had affairs; how to discern which couples you can treat and which you can't; and how to have hope for those couples who feel absolutely hopeless themselves.

All the chapters include composite case studies taken from our years of clinical work with couples. Although individual details have been combined and altered, the themes of their treatment remain true.

In these pages we hope to convince you that working with couples is enormously gratifying and perhaps not as difficult as you may think. The principles we outline can be applied to great effect with a little practice. Once you have tried them, we hope that you'll have an experience similar to ours: To travel with your couples as week by week their compassion for each other deepens, their hurt feelings recede, and the ashes of their passion miraculously come back to life.

There's nothing more fulfilling in therapy than watching two people find each other again. When you hear them praise rather than curse each other, you know you're on the right track. When they cry about the pain they've caused each other, you're getting there. When they can laugh at each other's foibles rather than raging about them, your work is nearly finished. When they leave your office hand in hand, you've made it. An added bonus? Their kids will be happier, too. They won't have to duck into their bedrooms to shut out the yelling they hear downstairs. Instead, as they come downstairs for breakfast, they'll catch their parents kissing. What's better than that? You'll know that you've helped bring a little more love into the world.

We hope that with the help of these principles, you will find your way to treating couples with a sure and steady hand. It is a journey worth taking.

Acknowledgments

We thank our beloved friend Etana Kunovsky for her tireless dedication to co-creating and sustaining the Gottman Institute since its inception. Without her, our work would never have reached beyond office and lab. Deep gratitude also goes to Alan Kunovsky for his brilliant skill and integrity in taking over the helm of the Gottman Institute. We also thank Katie Reynolds who has guided us in all our travels, ensuring smooth landings and flourishing relationships wherever we go. Our sincere gratitude goes to Linda Wright, the Institute Director of Couples' Services, who has personally spoken with thousands of distressed people and ushered them to our workshops, and to our Institute's Clinical Director, David Penner, for his calm and conscientious leadership. Laura Heck and Allie Wood in the Institute's Training Department have flawlessly coordinated hundreds of workshops for clinicians, and in the products department, Belinda Gray and Kyle Morrison have designed and provided materials for couples and clinicians. Our thanks go to them. Our deep appreciation also goes to Michael Fulwiler, Ellie

Lisitsa, and Keeley Trygstad for shepherding us into a new technological world.

We also wish to thank Deborah Malmud at W. W. Norton and Company for her unwavering faith in this project and her unerring editorial eye, and Rafael Lisitsa, whose comments and insight proved invaluable. Also many thanks to our beloved friends who supported us throughout: Alison Shaw, Derk Jager, Marten Jager, Phillip and Cara Cohn, Denise and James Wolf, Kathryn Crawford, Carol Parks, Mavis Tsai, and Lana Lisitsa. And as always, great appreciation goes to our daughter, Moriah Gottman, who has patiently listened to endless hours of research results and clinical stories over the years and given us her joy, laughter, and insight.

Finally, to all the clinicians who have believed in our work at the Gottman Institute and have dedicated themselves to repairing and restoring families worldwide, we give our deepest gratitude.

10 PRINCIPLES
for Doing Effective Couples Therapy

INTRODUCTION
Facing the Gauntlet

It's Monday. Time to begin your week seeing couples smart enough to seek help before it's too late. You've hung up your coat, flicked on the lights, straightened the papers on your desk, and set your notepad and pens beside you. You're ready to begin.

You crack open the door to the waiting room and the tension is as thick as the smoke from a four-alarm fire. That must be the new couple. They sit on either side of an empty chair, a bad sign. He's reading the *Wall Street Journal*. With a navy blazer, black glasses, pale striped shirt, and cobalt blue tie, he's every inch the businessman. He frowns as he turns the pages.

Two chairs away his wife is staring into space, a grimace on her face. Maybe 50, she's sleek but tense, tilted forward, her shields up and ready for battle.

They could be strangers. They're not. They're your next couple.

Married for 27 years, they've barely spoken for 20. Once you invite them in, each will tug on you to take their side until you feel like a rubber band. You'll get to hear them cut each other to ribbons, rage over age-old betrayals, and charge each other with crimes so heinous you suddenly feel black-robed like a courtroom judge.

Welcome to couples therapy.

No wonder most therapists shy away from couples work. Even Sigmund Freud tried it once, but dropped it with scalded hands. He thought he could individually psychoanalyze both spouses in separate sessions during the same week. Apparently he hated the experience so much that in 1919 he wrote a paper condemning it and recommended that no psychoanalyst ever try to help any couple.

Today couples therapy has lost some of its burning edges. Extensive research by John and later both of us plus studies by other scientists have unlocked the secrets of how couples succeed or fail in creating lasting relationships. Based on John's studies begun over 40 years ago, together with our summed 55 years of clinical experience (John for 15; Julie for 40), we have designed a couples therapy method and trained over 25,000 clinicians in it worldwide.

When first creating our theory and therapy method, we were married in both home and work life. Supposedly the perfect collegial duo, we fought like cats and dogs. Should the therapy be prescriptive, fourteen sessions sharply outlined and standardized, a number John preferred? Or more tailored to the couple at hand, handling not only relationship dynamics but individual tribulations too? How about each partner's childhood history? Doesn't it season his or her behavior? What if he's drinking? Or she's over the moon about their next door neighbor? How do you do *that* in 14 sessions? Over the years we treated hundreds of cases, discussed them heatedly over dinner (which bored our daughter to tears), and slowly refined our work into a blend of research-based clinical work and clinical-based research.

The result is the subject of this book, the 10 principles we believe make a good couples therapist.

Couples therapy can be like traversing a minefield. Take a wrong step and you can blow up someone's trauma history. A wrong step and you can be met with a glare of disapproval. A wrong step and he can say, "See, she even agrees with me," and that's even worse. Another wrong step and they can fall into stunned silence, both feeling scolded by you. It makes you hesitant to even step out the door. What's a therapist to do?

We try to do our best, which is not always perfect.

A note before we begin: We are not here to tell you how we alone know how to do couples therapy with infallible methods that guarantee you fortune, fame, and hundreds of grateful clients. You're much smarter than that—you know it's not that simple.

What we want to give you is a very humble and human guide to the practice of couples therapy. Practice, not perfection. It's like trying to master a Bach suite on the cello. You can work on it for years. You can have masterful days when you soar with wisdom. And terrible days when you think about that alternate profession. You know the one, the fantasy you keep tucked away just for days like this: Wouldn't it be great to be a gardener and spend lovely days outside? Wouldn't it be great to be an interior decorator and not risk kids growing up with the ruins of divorce? Oh right, spousal conflicts about decorating decisions can also cause World War III. There's no perfect alternative.

We know you have many questions. When you're with your couples, what events should you focus on? Which events should you ignore? How do you avoid getting drawn into the conflict? What if you like him more than you like her? What if you can't empathize with either one of them? How do you guide the session, and towards what end? What if you want to exit stage left every time the Joneses are due to arrive?

Our answers will be both technical and personal. This book will touch on research-based methods that are tried and tested, but will hopefully extend beyond these.

We will tell you stories that reveal our fears, fumblings, failures, and successes as we detail the journeys we've taken with drowning couples seeking a peaceful shore to share. We want this book to be a treasure chest for you, full of tangled gold coins, jewels, and delights. As we sort through the contents, there may be some duds we have to toss: some coins that, when bitten down on, bend and break like the thin tin of fakery. But as we examine each principle and hold it up to the light, hopefully they'll glow for you as they have for us. Best of all, maybe they'll light up your own wisdom and truths and help you become the best couples therapist you can be.

We want to help you approach couples therapy with hope and confidence, not trepidation and quaking. We've settled on 10 principles we think are the most helpful and that apply to all kinds of therapy approaches. They're actually not difficult. If we can do them, so can you. They stem from all those years we've spent with couples in the lab and in the consulting office. Those triumphant or troubled souls have taught us everything we know.

Couples are marvelous teachers. With every sigh, rolled eye, and glaring glance they show us what to do and what not to do. If we therapists are having a good day and manage to get most of it right, they bless us with a smile and a nod. Their voices drop down a few decibels and take on a softer lilt. They may even grab hold of each other's hands and grin at each other. For us, that's the best reward of all.

Here is the summary of what those many couples have taught us. We hope we get it right.

1

THE FIRST PRINCIPLE

Use Research-Based Methods to Treat Couples

Science differentiates truth from fiction. The psychotherapy field is no exception. These days we hear that our methods should be rooted in scientific study. After all, research in psychology and neuroscience has made tremendous strides over the past five decades, especially in the causes and treatment of psychopathology.

Before scientists zeroed in on mental illness, we thought poor mothering was the cause of almost every disorder. We assumed that cold, distant mothers created autism, and mothers giving double messages spawned schizophrenia. But later, studies in genetics and neuroscience corrected these misconceptions. It turned out moms weren't so bad; broken DNA and crossed wiring were more the problem.

Recently there have been thousands of studies on what works and doesn't in individual psychotherapy treatment. Now we know that for many people, cognitive therapy eases depression, behavioral desensitization cures phobias, and medication helps contain psychoses. As therapists we look to these methods to help our clients because they have been scientifically validated and have proven helpful. But what methods do we use when it comes to treating couples? Let's look at the history of our field first to understand the context in which scientific studies have been conducted and what they have taught us.

In psychology, it began in the mid-twentieth century. The 1950s and '60s were revolutionary years in American intellectual history, a time of turmoil, upheaval, and immense creativity. Innovation replaced stale thinking in nearly every field, and psychotherapy was no exception. Up until then, psychoanalysis had been the gold standard for treatment. But now new visionaries like Fritz Perls, R. D. Laing, B. F. Skinner, Albert Ellis, Carl Rogers, and Victor Frankl broke free of Freudian constraints, creating new therapies that focused on the here-and-now instead of the there-and-then.

The identity of who needed treatment morphed as well. Pioneers like Virginia Satir, Murray Bowen, Paul Watzlawick, Salvador Minuchin, and Jay Haley birthed a new field—therapy for couples and families. These thinkers tried to pinpoint relationship dynamics that disrupted smooth family functioning and then designed interventions to change them. Each was brilliant. Yet none of these greats paused to scientifically study the relationships they treated. Instead, they observed as best they could, conceptualized what they saw, and plunged forward into formulating treatments.

Minuchin was particularly prescient. He said, "Every marriage is a mistake. It's how you deal with it that matters." He presaged John's later finding that all couples have perpetual unresolvable problems they must learn to live with. Minuchin thought misplaced boundaries within the family cause dysfunction, and therapy should focus on realigning them.

Paul Watzlawick, Gregory Bateson, and Don Jackson spotted hidden meanings and agendas lurking under the surface of family communications and figured these were the problem. They designed ways to fish these meta-communications out of the depths and into the open where they could be more directly discussed.

Ideas like these became the cornerstones of family therapy. But some contained serious flaws not spotted until later, when they were scientifically scrutinized. In their book *The Mirages of Marriage*, Lederer and Jackson based their couples' treatment on a theory called "Quid Pro Quo." They thought healthy marriages were those where one partner responds to the other's good behavior with his or her own good behavior in turn. Marriages managed reciprocally would succeed, whereas those lacking in reciprocity would fail. Based on reciprocity theory, they proposed that the cure for ailing relationships was to help couples establish a contingency contract, an agreement in which each spouse "gives to get."

For years no one tested this theory's validity. Finally a decade later Bernard Murstein put contingency contracting under the microscope. His research revealed that relationships based on reciprocity are actually ailing and failing, not healthy as Lederer and Jackson had presumed. The spouses who tally up the good they do versus the good their partners do are in fact quite unhappy. They are like affect accountants, with thoughts like, "I did this great thing for her, but she never reciprocated." In truth couples in happy relationships rarely give reciprocity a second thought. Murstein found that people do good for their partners because they simply love them and want what is best for them, not to get something in return.

When treating couples, if we embraced reciprocity theory and encouraged couples to create a contract with one another, imagine what could happen. Chances are good they would remain miserable. Then we'd be left thinking either we were bad therapists (always a possibility) or our clients were impossible to help (less likely). The real glitch would probably be in the method itself.

In the mid-1960s, George Bach presented another treatment approach in his book *The Intimate Enemy*. Bach emphasized that couples should always air their resentments by "letting it rip" rather than allowing them to build up. This way they clear the air. He believed so strongly in this concept that he even encouraged partners to express themselves by hitting each other with foam rubber bats called *batakas*.

If we practiced his methods, a session of his might look like this:

JILL: "I hate it that you never help me with the housework!" *Whap!*

JACK: "Well, we never have enough sex and you're a lousy lover!" *Whap!*

Not surprisingly, later studies countered Bach's approach. It turned out that airing resentments has no cathartic effect. Venting doesn't diminish anger; it increases it. Bach did have a point, however. We know that suppressing anger isn't the answer either. Bottling up anger can lead to depression, withdrawal, bitterness, even a dampened immune system. But anger isn't the enemy. Anger is hard-wired into our brains. It is a normal and natural response when we are treated unfairly or blocked from achieving a goal. Minus physical or verbal attacks, couples do need ways to raise and listen to each other's complaints. Bach's mistake was to *only* focus on airing resentments (plus perhaps the batakas). Research has revealed that much more is needed.

Murray Bowen embraced the opposite approach. He thought all negative emotions like anger are destructive and interfere with problem solving. Couples must remain calm, cool, and collected—in short, completely rational, for if they let loose their feelings, all hell will break loose. Then nothing can be achieved. In other words, emotion is the enemy that mucks up the marital work of problem solving. In Bowen's world rationality is good and emotion not so good. The therapist's job is to make sure partners remain calm by helping them rein in their unruly emotions. Then a healthy rational dialogue can follow.

Bowen also pointed out that the healthiest couples are less "enmeshed" and more "differentiated." The more separate and independent they are from each other, the better. Dependency, he claimed, is dysfunctional. It goes hand in hand with being too emotional. So according to Bowen, couples should work on being less dependent, simmer down their emotions, and become more rational.

Again later studies undermined these ideas. Research in neuroscience showed that emotions are central to problem solving, not an obstacle to it. In fact, millions of neurons connect the brain's limbic system or center for emotions with the frontal cortex or the executive problem-solving area of the brain. Kahneman and Tversky showed there are two kinds of thinking. One enables rapid intuitive thinking (they called it Type 1 thinking) and the other, a slower rational thinking (Type 2 thinking). The neurologist Antonio Damasio wrote that a patient of his had a tumor removed from his frontal cortex and was afterwords unable to prioritize his options, think creatively, or problem solve. These scientists demonstrated that without access to our emotions, our rational processes are handicapped, and we become little better than a conglomeration of arbitrary and random behaviors.

Regarding Bowen's disdain for dependency, how could our species have survived through the mists of time without it? Biologically we are pack animals. For at least 250,000 years we have lived collectively. Communal cooperation has enabled us to survive centuries of ice, famine, and the teeth of hungry predators. Without depending on each other, our species would have perished long ago. With good reason we say, "No man or woman stands alone."

Science has substantiated the value of interdependency. Medical research has demonstrated that when patients depend on others and are not alone, they recover faster and better from a whole host of problems, including heart attacks, strokes, and cancer. Psychological studies have also shown that people who are in committed relationships tend to live longer and are happier and more successful than those who live alone. In addition, sociologists have found that people who possess greater social capital, that is, networks of others they depend on, report greater life satisfaction than those with little social capital. There's little doubt that interdependency has distinct life-giving benefits.

Scientific studies did well at exposing the myths about relationships. But it wasn't until the 1970s that anyone actually observed couples' relationships to discover the truth of why some relationships succeeded while others failed. Up until then, most studies had relied on partners filling out questionnaires or supplying self-reports. But these methods were littered with flaws and bias. There were still no valid answers to explain the course of relationships.

John had recently earned his doctorate and was teaching psychology at Indiana University where he met a colleague who became his best friend, Robert Levenson. At the time their respective romantic relationships weren't going so well. For the time being, they figured it might be better to study romantic relationships rather than have them.

John hoped to understand relationships well enough to predict their future course. Why did some couples end up on the high road towards marital success? What made others fall to the doomed road below that dead-ended in divorce?

John began his research in 1972. Before then only seven studies had tried to predict the future of couples' relationships. One investigator had examined partners' wardrobes to see if their clothing choices predicted future marital satisfaction. The study found that wives with nice wardrobes would have happier relationships, but nice clothes made no difference for husbands. Imagine a therapy based on this study: "Jane, you should go shopping. But for you, Jack, those sweats are fine."

Clearly there was more to learn. But John had to fight an uphill battle to do observational research. His colleagues argued it was hard enough to observe reliable patterns of behavior in one person. Observing interactions in two would only square the data's statistical unreliability, thus making the study of couples pointless. John persisted anyway.

First he observed university student couples. While they discussed a problem they were having for 15 minutes, he videotaped and coded their interactions using a system he and his graduate student, Cliff Notarius invented, the Couples' Interaction Scoring System (CISS). Later on, another student of his replicated the study with couples in rural Indiana. In both studies the types of communication patterns observed were nearly identical.

Next John built a "talk table" with a rating dial that ranged from positive to negative. While discussing an issue, the device enabled partners to rate the intention of their own responses as well as the impact of their partner's responses. Using statistics designed to study sequences of interaction, again John found extremely reliable patterns in couples' thoughts and interactions.

In 1976, John and Robert Levenson teamed up. Levenson brought to the research a specialized knowledge of psychophysiology and its measurement that was added to the rating dial procedures. In the lab, couples were wired up to instruments that measured heart rate, sweat gland production, blood velocity, and overall bodily movement. These measurements were synched to the video time code. Then the couples were asked to discuss a conflict issue for 15 minutes. For some couples, as they became upset their physiological measurements rocketed into the stratosphere. They might have looked calm on the outside but inside, their heart rates would jump to 100–150 beats per minute. Their hands would sweat, their blood would race, and their bodies would jiggle. These data indicated that they were experiencing an attack. In the moment the partner facing them resembled a saber-toothed tiger with fangs bared. In response, they shifted into diffuse physiological arousal (DPA), a state of fight-or-flight.

Afterward the couples watched their videotapes and rated the emotional responses they recalled having during their discussion. Then they returned home. To find out how these couples fared, three years later they were re-contacted and asked to return to the lab where the same procedures were repeated.

John, Levenson, and their colleagues were astounded. In other studies that tried to predict behavior, correlations between the best personality measures and behavior hovered around 0.10 to 0.30. This meant that by measuring personality at Time 1, scientists could predict Time 2 behavior with only 9% accuracy. But by measuring couples' behavior, rating dials, and physiology at Time 1, Gottman and Levenson could accurately predict the changes in the couples' marital satisfaction three years later with 90% accuracy. Numbers like that were unheard of in psychology research. It turned out that diffuse physiological arousal during conflict discussion was an especially powerful predictor of relationship demise in the future, along with several other factors.

In the same study couples were also asked to have an events-of-the-day discussion before talking about a conflict. By analyzing the two discussions together, more patterns emerged. When husbands showed disinterest or lacked positive emotions in the events-of-the-day discussion, their wives tended to complain more harshly in the conflict discussion that followed. The quality of the couple's friendship, especially how well the husband maintained it, predicted the quality of the couple's ability to manage conflict.

For the next series of studies John fine-tuned his observational coding methods and analytic processes. Based on Paul Ekman and Wallace Friesen's Facial Affect Coding System, he created the Specific Affect Coding System (SPAFF) plus new methods of sequential and time-series analysis that enabled deeper description and understanding of change over time.

The original studies were then replicated and expanded to follow newlyweds through their transition into parenthood. Together with Levenson, John also studied the relationships of gay and lesbian couples for 12 years and older heterosexual couples through retirement for as long as 20 years, thanks to Levenson's tenacity. In addition, John joined with his colleague, Neil Jacobson to study violent couples for nine years. Once again, most of the findings replicated.

Meanwhile, in 1986, John and I serendipitously moved from different corners of the country to Seattle. Shortly afterwards we met each other and in 1987 we married. Now we could benefit from all that research of John's not only professionally, but personally too.

We joined forces to build an apartment lab at the University of Washington so we could observe more than 15-minute lab discussions. Newlywed couples were asked to spend 24 hours in the apartment as they might in a bed-and-breakfast, as they pleased. Then they were followed up and observed annually for the next six years.

The atmosphere in the apartment was soothing with just a few exceptions: There were three cameras bolted to the walls, a one-way window, staff personnel who observed the couple from behind the window, and other staff who took occasional blood and urine samples from each partner. Other than that, it was like a perfectly restful vacation spot.

Most couples ate, read, watched TV, talked, and slept. John's student, Janice Driver spent years working in the apartment lab, trying to ferret out what predicted sustained friendship and intimacy in these newlyweds. Driver was particularly intrigued by the minutiae of their smallest exchanges—the turn of a head, a mumbled monosyllable, a focused eye gaze. She wanted to know, when one partner made a bid for connection by calling the other person's name or commenting on something, would that elicit the other partner's interested response, or something else? After a decade, she and John figured out that the smallest moments told an important story. The particular ways partners responded to each other's bids for connection forged the relative strength of their future friendship and intimacy, which in turn shaped how well they managed conflict. It was like the effect of water on rock. If waves of water emptily lapped away at the base of a rock, eventually it would weaken and collapse with erosion. But if the waves continually deposited new silt at the rock's base, over time the rock would grow stronger and capable of withstanding the big storms ahead.

The newlyweds who remained happily married six years later turned towards each other's bids an average of 86% of the time compared with 33% of the time for those destined to divorce. It only took a few words to make all the difference. If one partner said, "It's tough reading all the bad news in the paper," and the other said, "Yeah, it sure is," that relationship was much more likely to succeed than one with no response. Silence or turning away from a bid was like a death knell for the relationship. Worst still were the marriages where the partner turned against the other's bid with exclamations like, "Be quiet! Can't you see I'm busy?" In sum, these small moments of turning towards each other's bids for connection were crucial for relationship happiness. Even if a hurricane assaulted a marriage, these moments built the foundation that kept it from toppling into the sea.

Taken together the couples we studied who generously gave us their time put a crystal ball into our hands. Across all the studies, we had learned enough to watch a couple at Time 1 and accurately predict with better than 90% accuracy whether they would separate or divorce six years later. Once that news came out, people we didn't know very well stopped inviting us for dinner.

All in all, we have studied more than 3,000 couples and participated in studies of 3,500 more. Here is a summary of everything our couples have taught us.

First, there are four big predictors of relationship demise. We call them the Four Horsemen of the Apocalypse, after the biblical harbingers of doom.

The first Horseman is criticism. If partners regularly use criticism to voice their complaints where one partner blames a problem on the other partner's character flaws, the relationship will slowly sink. Words like "You never wash the dishes!" or "You're so selfish" only inspire resentment, not cooperation or care.

The second Horseman is contempt. This one leads couples to gallop over a cliff. Partners who are contemptuous act superior and punctuate their criticisms with a sneer, a left lip corner raise, or an eye roll that signifies their superiority and disgust. They may also mock their partner or use sarcasm, like, "Aw, your pinkie hurts? Poor baby. Guess that gets you out of doing the dishes . . .

again." When partners bludgeon each other with contempt, it not only destroys relationship happiness, it also shreds the listening partner's immune system. The number of times one partner hears the other partner's contempt during a 15-minute conflict discussion predicts how many infectious illnesses the listener will have the following year. Contempt quickly destroys relationships.

Partners who respond to each other with the third Horseman, defensiveness, are also riding roughshod towards demise. Defensiveness goes hand in hand with criticism and contempt, since few partners can withstand being trampled without wanting to defend themselves. When being defensive, partners may either play the innocent victim, as in, "I do the dishes all the time. Why are you being so mean?" or they can counterattack, as in, "You're a fine one to talk. When was the last time you paid the bills?" This is the toughest communication habit to eradicate.

The fourth Horseman we call stonewalling. Gottman and Levenson found that when partners become physiologically aroused during conflict discussions with heart rates above 100 beats per minute, they often shut down all verbal responses, divert their gaze, and turn their bodies away, thus blocking out their partners and becoming in effect a stone wall. Slamming into walls is terrible for a relationship.

These Four Horsemen bear bad tidings for a relationship. In fact, couples plagued by them divorce an average of 5.6 years after the wedding. On the other hand, we find that almost everyone uses them from time to time (including us). But the difference between happy couples who are relationship masters and unhappy couples who are relationship disasters is that master couples make repairs; disaster couples do not. Relationship masters don't sweep bad fights or regrettable incidents under the rug and pretend they never happened. Instead, they return to them, talk about them, and to try to understand them. They listen to each other's feelings and points of view. They figure out what they each did wrong. Then they take responsibility for what they regret saying or doing and apologize. When regrettable incidents are processed like this, they lose their destructive force, like a typhoon that is grounded and halted by moving inland.

Our Four Horsemen are not the only powerful predictors we found. Positive interactions count, too, especially during conflict. When discussing a problem, if partners express understanding and empathy or smile or make a small repair or say something funny, their relationships are likely to succeed. Relationships fare much better when their ratio of positive to negative interactions during conflict is at least five to one, that is, their positive interactions outnumber their negative interactions by five to one. Relationships destined to fail have an average ratio of 0.8 to 1, or around one positive interaction for every negative one. During nonconflict times, the ratio that predicts success is much higher, around 20 to 1. Clearly relationships need rich bank accounts of positive interaction to survive and thrive. During conflict husbands and wives each have important roles to play for their relationships to do well. Wives who raise their complaints gently without blame and criticism tend to have sunnier futures, while husbands who accept influence from their wives benefit, too. The *Los Angeles Times* coined this finding for husbands the "Yes, dear," phenomenon.

As they collected data over longer time spans, John and Levenson also found another pattern that predicted divorce. There was a group of couples who didn't have the Four Horsemen during conflict. Instead, they showed an emotional disengagement, a lack of responsiveness, and low levels of positive emotions during conflict. Couples who were emotionally disengaged divorced an average of 16.2 years after the wedding.

Now that all the moving parts were identified, the predictors of relationship success or failure, it was time to build a theory for what it takes to make a relationship succeed. But for a theory to be valid, it has to be testable or disconfirmable. That is the hallmark of good science. Testing theory in our field requires clinical interventions.

In 1996 we began to explore what would happen if we taught distressed couples the same skills successful couples displayed in their relationships. We started with simple steps called proximal change studies. This tested the power of one intervention to change a poor conversation to a better one the second time around.

We first tried out a couple's intervention for physiological arousal. After one or both partners moved into fight-or-flight responses during a conflict discussion, a staff person entered the room, told the couple there was a problem with the equipment, and asked them to move temporarily to the waiting room. They were instructed to read a magazine and not talk to each other. After 20 minutes, they were summoned back to the lab and asked to continue their conflict discussion. In reality nothing was wrong with the equipment. The break in the discussion was designed to slow their heart rates and dissipate their stress to see if a break and self-soothing could convert an escalated quarrel into a calm and constructive discussion. The intervention worked. Physiologically aroused couples with no break listened badly and ended up trampling each other with the Four Horsemen. But when another group of couples took a break, in the second discussion they spoke with more care, listened to one another, expressed empathy, and worked towards compromise. The differences between the pre- and post-break discussions were so dramatic it looked like partners had undergone a brain transplant.

Two other proximal studies were conducted with John's graduate students, Kim Ryan and Amber Tabares. These studies also demonstrated that it was possible to change couples' interactions using very brief interventions.

By combining the results of these and other studies we had enough to validate our theory, called the Sound Relationship House (SRH).

Nine building blocks make up the Sound Relationship House—seven floors that are supported by two walls. The following describes them:

- **BUILD LOVE MAPS:** The bottom floor refers to the importance of partners knowing each other's psychological worlds well enough to map them. Each partner's inner world is composed of needs, values, past experiences, priorities, stresses, and so on. As partners evolve over time, their love maps change. To build and keep love maps updated, relationship masters ask each other questions, especially open-ended ones.
- **SHARE FONDNESS AND ADMIRATION:** The second floor creates a culture of appreciation that supplies a relationship's emotional bank account with assets. Most important at

FIGURE 1.1 The Sound Relationship House. Copyright © 2000–2015 by Dr. John Gottman and Dr. Julie Schwartz Gottman. Distributed under license by The Gottman Institute, Inc.

this level is partners not only feeling love and admiration but also expressing it often.

- **TURNING TOWARDS VERSUS AWAY:** The third floor is built from those small moments when partners make a bid for each other's attention and connection. Relationship masters turn towards most of their partners' bids rather than away or against their partner.

These first three floors of the SRH determine how well couples maintain their friendship, intimacy, and passion. The next floor up is an add-on that results from the relative strengths of the lower three floors plus the floor above it.

- **POSITIVE PERSPECTIVE:** This level is based on the work of Robert Weiss at the University of Oregon. Weiss observed that couples could either be in positive sentiment override (what we call the "positive perspective") or negative sentiment override (or "negative perspective"). *Positive perspective* refers to an overall feeling partners have about each other in which one partner's positive sentiments outweigh the negative response he or she may have to the other's occasional bad behavior. If a husband wakes up grumpy, a wife with positive perspective will figure he just had a bad night's sleep, whereas with negative perspective, she will think he is being mean. Positive or negative perspective is determined by the relative strength of the couple's friendship plus how well they manage conflict. This floor cannot be worked on directly, but it can be influenced by changes in the other SRH levels. A strong friendship and good conflict management skills help ensure the positive perspective.

The next two floors of the SRH are fundamental to good conflict management.

- **MANAGE CONFLICT:** There are six skills that form this floor. The first one is how a complaint is raised. Voicing a complaint with a softened start-up rather than criticism or contempt works best. In a softened start-up, the partner describes him- or herself rather than naming a negative trait of the other person's. The start-up usually begins with "I feel . . ." as in, "I feel worried about the bills not getting paid," rather than words like, "You are so . . . (lazy, irresponsible, etc.)." The second skill is whether partners accept influence from each other when working towards a compromise. Accepting influence is a strength for both men and women. Third is a couple's ability to make repairs in the middle of a conversation when it begins to skid downhill—the sooner, the better. Fourth is a couple's ability to de-escalate a quarrel after the Four Horsemen have taken over the lead. Fifth is each partner's ability to self-soothe before their physiological arousal explodes their discussion into chaos. Couples who do this well take a break from the conversation in order to calm down. The sixth skill is crucial when all else fails: the couple's ability to process and recover from a regrettable incident or bad fight.

- **MAKE LIFE DREAMS COME TRUE:** Most individuals have dreams, hopes, and aspirations. Couples who honor each other's dreams and support each other to fulfill them have relationships that are nearly unbreakable. Our research revealed that when a couple gets gridlocked on an issue and can't get near resolving it, each partner may have a dream at the core of their position that hasn't been aired or understood yet. When partners disclose these dreams to one another, their rigid opposition often melts away which smoothes the way towards compromise.

The top floor of the SRH is also the deepest one. It gets at the heart of each partner's world.

- **CREATE SHARED MEANING:** Life experience etches into every individual a unique set of values and beliefs. It isn't essential that partners share exactly the same ones, although some overlap is helpful. More important is that couples can talk about them with each other. Couples strong in shared meaning discuss questions like what purpose gives each of their lives meaning and what legacies they want to leave behind. Nothing is left in the dark. Because this level relies on good Love Mapping, it circles us back to the bottom level of the SRH, where Love Mapping lives. John likes to say the SRH is really more like a bagel.

The seven levels of the SRH stand strong when the two walls supporting them are solid. The walls are Trust and Commitment.

- *Trust* refers to each partner knowing that the other partner will be there for them in a host of ways: When they are sad, angry, frightened, humiliated, overweight, underweight, triumphant, defeated, joyous, despairing, sick, broken, helpless, hopeful, dream-filled, and so on. Trust is erected by one partner choosing to show up for the other—not perfectly, not every time, but as much as one can.
- Commitment is about loyalty, cherishing one's partner above all others, not scanning the horizon for who might be better. Commitment doesn't always imply marriage,

> given that some partners don't feel it necessary to legally formalize their commitment, and in some places, partners are forbidden to marry even if they want to. But with or without a legal document, *commitment* means a life-long promise of devotion and care. Where there is commitment, there is no worry of being replaced if someone "better" comes along.

Once the SRH theory was fleshed out and established, it was time to take it out for a clinical dry run. We combined our best proximal change interventions into a two-day psychoeducational workshop for couples called the Art and Science of Love. Gottman Couples Therapy became the clinical application of the collected interventions. Kim Ryan tested the efficacy of both the workshop and the therapy in a randomized clinical trial with one-year follow-up. She found that days one and two of the workshop proved more successful at helping couples than either day alone, but most effective longitudinally was the workshop followed by nine sessions of Gottman Couples Therapy.

Next we tackled the question of what happens to young couples after their first babies arrive. The results shocked us. After the happy event, 67% of couples experienced a precipitous decline in relationship satisfaction during the first three years of the baby's life. John's student Alyson Shapiro compared the 33% of couples who didn't experience this downturn in satisfaction with the 67% of couples who did, which enabled an intervention to be empirically designed for the stricken couples.

We created a two-day workshop called Bringing Baby Home

(BBH), and then performed a randomized clinical trial with long-term follow-up to test its effectiveness. Again, the research bore fruit. The workshop reversed the decline in satisfaction couples experienced after their baby was born, leaving them happier and less burdened by hostile conflicts. In addition, it curtailed the development of postpartum depression in mothers.

BBH came to the attention of the federal Administration of Children and Families. In 2003, we were asked to design a curriculum similar to BBH but this time for unmarried couples having their first baby while struggling with poverty.

On a personal note, in my first 20 years of postgraduate work, therapy with the disadvantaged had been my first love. The mentally ill in an Oregon hospital, heroin addicts in the Boston "combat zone," Vietnam veterans in skid-row Los Angeles, and incest survivor women trapped by their trauma had taught me a lot about the suffering poverty creates. The wounds of trauma, addiction, broken families, and childhood abandonment had to be recognized and integrated into whatever we came up with.

The curriculum was encapsulated in 21 separate modules. Each one focused on a topic pertinent to relationships, parenting, or poverty. Small groups of couples met weekly with two trained facilitators who presented a different module each week. The group first watched a short videotaped talk show of an interview either John or I had conducted with impoverished couples on that week's topic. The shows were designed to foster group discussion in which the couples were encouraged to share their questions, experiences, and wisdom. Afterward the facilitators presented a brief teaching and gave the couples a relevant exercise to improve their friendship, intimacy, parenting, or conflict management skills. The curriculum was called Loving Couples Loving Children (LCLC).

A group based in Washington, DC, called Mathematica Social Policy and Research evaluated LCLC in a randomized clinical trial with 3,500 couples. With limited measures used, some effectiveness was demonstrated, especially with African American couples.

In our most recent study to date, we have applied a version of LCLC to couples plagued by episodes of situational domestic violence. Research by other scientists has shown that one out of every three couples has at least one violent episode before marriage, with more afterward. Their domestic violence can be categorized as either situational or characterological. Situational domestic violence is less severe, does not cause injury, tends to be symmetrical with both partners acting violently, and results in both partners expressing remorse and desire to change. Characterological violence looks very different. One partner is the perpetrator (most of the time, the male) and the other is the victim. The perpetrator feels no remorse and often blames the victim for his behavior, although there is nothing the victim can do to influence the course of the violence. In John and Neil Jacobson's nine-year study of domestically violent couples, they found that 80% of the couples were situationally violent while the remaining 20% were characterologically violent. Situational violence usually erupted during escalated quarrels that skidded off the rails. In contrast, characterological violence was used to enforce the perpetrator's power and control over the victim. It looked like the victims of characterological violence were the ones who most often wound up in battered women's shelters.

We despaired of ever helping characterological batterers and their partners, at least over the long haul. But we thought situational domestic violence might be remedied if couples could deepen their connection and learn emotion-focused conflict management skills, especially how to stay calm during conflict discussions. LCLC became the foundation of a new program called Couples Together Against Violence (CTAV). Four new modules were added to the curriculum that delved more deeply into anger management and the old emotional wounds that had generated the anger. We also incorporated the use of the Emwave, a biofeedback device that had been developed by a company called Heart Math. Each week before doing an exercise to strengthen the relationship, couples were asked to practice using the Emwave for five minutes in order to begin their work in a calm state of mind.

Our randomized clinical trial study with 18-month follow-up showed CTAV to be effective. For the couples studied, the program stopped all domestic violence, improved conflict management skills, deepened friendship and intimacy, and improved relationship satisfaction. These effects were lasting.

There is so much more to learn. But at this point, we can confidently say that science has helped us understand what makes relationships succeed or fail. Our therapy and workshops that are based on research seem to also work for a majority of couples, at least better than partners hitting each other with batakas. They especially work when learned and practiced early on. Our point is that if you want to do couples therapy, you will be far more effective if you equip yourself with research-based methods, whether they are ours or those of others.

So we come to our first principle for doing effective couples therapy: Use research-based methods to treat couples.

The couples we see are often in terrible distress. Don't they deserve the best we can give them? Couples therapy, like any form of psychotherapy, is an art form at its best. But underlying the art, there needs to be methods built on the truth of what couples need to succeed rather than those based in myths patched together out of stereotypes. And science is the avenue that can best lead us towards truth.

Bringing It Into Practice

- Research-based methods work best to treat couples effectively.
- The Sound Relationship House theory describes what it takes to build a strong relationship.
- The Four Horsemen of the Apocalypse—criticism, contempt, defensiveness and stonewalling—predict relationship demise.
- Diffuse physiological arousal (a fight-or-flight response) leads to escalated quarrels and stonewalling.
- Successful couples remain calm when discussing conflicts.
- Successful relationships have a five to one ratio of positive to negative interactions during conflict.
- Situational domestic violence can be successfully treated using a couples group model.

THE SECOND PRINCIPLE

Assess First, Then Decide on Treatment

Sally is furious. Over the phone she tells me her husband is a cad. Every word is sharp and emphatic. She punches out a quick summary of their problem and asks for an appointment as soon as possible. I agree to see her and her husband the next day.

Sally's story is this: They had met with another therapist eight months ago. Sally thought her husband, Mark, was cheating on her during his business trips abroad. But the therapist thought otherwise. He soothed her fears. "You're just insecure because you've gained some weight, Sally, and Mark isn't pleased about that." At first she believed him, thinking she must be imagining things. After all, this wasn't the first time she'd misjudged someone. In her first go-round she had married a fellow she thought was great who within a year had a complete breakdown. It turned out he suffered from schizophrenia, but she hadn't known it. Her dreams of a happy future had ended the day he wrapped his hands around her neck and squeezed. It was a good thing she had escaped. Now again she was being told the opposite of her own view: "No worries. It'll all be okay." (If you lose some weight.) It felt placating. Her gut ached with that feeling—the one she would get in her first marriage whenever she ignored her fears, especially when they were screaming at her to pay attention. But here was a therapist and expert; he should know what he was talking about. She thought, "Okay. Maybe if I lose 10 pounds, everything will get better." But still, something didn't feel right.

More signs appeared. Too many missed dinners after work, too many missed calls when he was abroad, too many slammed-down laptop screens when she entered the room.

Two months ago she had hired an investigator, a non-descript little fellow with thick glasses who had a way of melting into the background. He followed Mark for six months. One week he hit the jackpot: a cache of secret e-mails to prostitutes, lovers, the special "one" in Bangkok, and finally, a film of doing the deed with some young lady in a San Francisco hotel. The detective showed Sally all of it.

Upon Mark's return home, she yelled, pitched everything within reach at him, slung her closetful of clothes into a suitcase, and stomped out.

He called, pleaded, denied, raged, then begged some more. She finally relented. One last try.

On the surface this case doesn't look very complicated. He has messed up. She has a right to her rage. Maybe she will forgive him eventually; maybe she won't. Either way, it is a long slog back to any sort of trust.

As I think about it, all my stereotypes pop up: "He's no good.

She should get rid of him. She deserves better than this." I'm seeing them tomorrow. By then I'd better put a clamp on my mouth.

The next day we meet. They sit with miles between them. His head is dropped; her back is rigid. He stares at the carpet. She glares at him. Their sullen silence could rip down my walls. Where do I start?

John and I know a very wise therapist, Andy Greendorfer. He once said to us, "Driving faster won't get you there any sooner if you don't know where you're going." How true. With this suffering couple, what do I do first? Nail him and soothe her? Or postpone dealing with the affairs and dig into their family-of-origin issues? Diagnose each partner's psychopathology? How can we know more about who these people are and what they've each contributed to their marriage imploding? Yes, there have been affairs. But is that all? Why affairs as the poison of choice? Why not just gut-ripping arguments or icy silence? What happened to their sex life? Or for that matter, just savoring coffee and pastry together? What pot-holed road brought them here? There's no way of knowing unless we assess before taking a single step into intervention.

Most of us would rather leave the room than not immediately intervene with a couple this distressed. They've suffered long enough; they shouldn't have to wait another minute. They desperately want our help.

But think of it this way. If you dropped in on your long-trusted doctor complaining of daily abdominal pain, imagine how you would feel if she simply glanced at your belly and said, "Ahh, I've got a fix for that. Just roll up your sleeve and I'll inject you with this remedy. You'll be better in a jiffy." Not a very comforting thought. Neither you nor your doctor would have any real idea what ailed you or whether this particular medicine would work for you. The truth is that your abdomen contains a variety of organs that keep you well fueled, as well as muscle and bone that keeps you upright. With only a glance how could your doctor identify the real culprit causing your pain and why the pain had erupted in the first place? As much as you might want immediate help, you would probably want your doctor to thoroughly examine your abdomen first before deciding which treatment was best for you. Once she had carefully diagnosed the source of your discomfort, her chosen remedy would stand a far better chance of helping you than a blind stab at a cure.

The doctor's injection is precisely what many of us still do with every troubled couple. We assume the needs of all couples are the same. Then we inject our cure-all, our particular brand of psychotherapy, before we know the precise challenges the couple in front of us faces. In short, we do exactly what Greendorfer counsels us not to do: We drive without planning where we are headed; we treat without pinpointing what to treat.

John and I think it makes far more sense to take our time and assess a couple's relationship carefully and rigorously so that we know which way we're driving, where the bumps are in the road, and what turns we must take to best serve our clients.

This is the second principle for doing good couples therapy: Assess first, then decide on treatment. This principle, of course, raises an obvious question: What exactly do we assess?

Let's return to John's research. As you may recall, during the 1970s through the 1990s, John and his graduate students spent countless hours examining the videotapes and physiology of the couples they had brought into the lab, especially the couples who had returned year after year so they could be examined anew. As we described in Chapter 1, they were asked each time to discuss a conflict or the events of their day while being videotaped and having various physiological measures taken. Then the content of their words and affects were codified and correlated with data from the other measures.

When John and his colleagues first examined the data from these studies, they looked like a big cloud of gnats on graph paper. But then John began to spot patterns. Certain points linked together across the graphs like jet trails. The lines defined patterns of correlation or factors that could differentiate one set of relationships from another. When these factors were mathematically evaluated across time, they could be used to predict the future success or failure of a relationship five years down the road with astonishing accuracy. But having a collection of factors wasn't enough.

In the rainy months that followed John and I sorted out how these ingredients could be unified into theory. As each one emerged, we added it to the pot, simmered the resulting mixture down to its essence, figured out what ingredient was missing, and added that to the mix next. Finally the recipe seemed right and we had our theory.

A theory was one thing, but clinical application, another. How could we use the theory's factors to determine the needs of any particular couple quickly without having to bring them into our lab? In 1992, a colleague of John's, Cliff Notarius, and his graduate student, Jane Buongiorno found that the average time couples wait to seek help after first feeling distressed is six years. Imagine discovering a suspicious lump and delaying a doctor's appointment for six years! By the time couples appear on our doorstep they are typically in terrible trouble; their marriage is falling out of the sky. Three out of four propellers may be sputtering in smoke with the fourth barely keeping the marriage above tree line.

For each couple we needed to figure out what was wrong, why it had gone wrong, and what repairs were needed to send their relationship safely skyward again.

John has always been a master of measurement as well as observation. Beginning in 1980, he worked on designing a set of written questionnaires. He wanted these questionnaires to accurately reflect how a couple was doing on each level of the Sound Relationship House, not how they *thought* they were doing. Once they were designed, he statistically evaluated each questionnaire for reliability and validity to make sure that couples with similar problems reliably answered the questions in the same way, and that their answers actually measured what they purported to measure. Only items that correlated with other trustworthy ways of measuring a level of the Sound Relationship House theory were kept; other weaker items were shed. The result was a set of questionnaires that provided a clear snapshot of how paired partners actually were doing on each Sound Relationship House level.

John also added to our assessment process a modified version of one of our best lab procedures. It was a standardized interview that asked couples about the history of their relationship, called the Oral History Interview (OHI). The answers couples supplied weren't as important as the way they voiced them. Kim Buehlman, who worked in John's lab, created a way to codify the process of how couples answered the OHI questions. For example she codified how much couples gloried in triumphing over their struggles, how much couples felt battered by chaos in their lives, and how much respect they still expressed when describing each other. When partners described their years together, the number of times they used the word *we* rather than the word *I* signaled how close they felt to each other. While charting their transition to parenthood, if their answers were full of fondness and admiration rather than a lack of them, their friendship and intimate lives were probably still intact. When asked what first attracted them to each other, if a husband answered, "Her beautiful eyes," rather than, "Her credit card", at least his passion was probably still on fire and not cold ash. Buehlman's coding of the OHI was able to predict future divorce or stability with a whopping 94% accuracy.

Since the original OHI was designed for research couples and usually took two hours to complete, it was too long to fit the confines of a clinical session. So we chose only a few of the best questions to include in the clinical interview and added Buehlman's valuable coding system to help assess the strength of the couple's friendship and intimate life.

The third component we added to our assessment process was the psychotherapeutic equivalent of a blood test. Towards the end of the first interview, a clinician would ask the couple to discuss an unresolved problem for 10 minutes while the therapist simply looked on like a fly on the wall, without intervening. If the clinician attached heart rate monitors or pulse oximeters to each partner before they started, he or she could also learn if partners were escalating into a fight-or-flight state during their discussion. If desired, the clinician could also videotape this discussion to serve as a baseline measure of conflict management prior to intervention.

In testing the couple's conflict sample, we found that although they started out on their best behavior, they quickly slipped into behaviors that were more real and telling. These opened a window into the couple's world at home and how well or poorly they managed conflict. If the partners launched into criticism, defensiveness, and blame, that picture revealed a very different story than their speaking calmly and gently to one another.

We studied our assessment processes and found that the combination of a couple's written questionnaire scores, OHI answers, and conflict management sample yielded an accurate profile of the strengths and weaknesses of the couple's Sound Relationship House. We could also use the data to inform our decisions about treatment. If the bottom three floors pertaining to the couple's friendship were solid but the floors related to conflict management contained cracks that could bring the whole edifice down, we would begin treatment with work on conflict management. But if the couple was emotionally miles apart and hadn't talked together in years, let alone worked on conflict issues, we would begin by helping them create new ways of routinely connecting with one another. If their friendship and conflict management looked fine but a difference in meaning and values was dividing them, that's where we would start. In other words, our assessment would serve as our compass. It would tell us where the relationship was off track and which turns to take to return the couple to a healthier path.

Fifteen years have passed since John and I designed this assessment process. New research findings have led to refinements, but its basic format has held up over time.

With assessment in mind, I begin my first session with Mark and Sally.

I ask them what brings them into therapy. What is each one's story? Mark tells me he came to this country from South America at age 18. At 28, he met Sally, fell in love, and they married. Together they created a successful business importing textiles. But things are bad now. Sally agrees. What do they want from therapy?

Mark says he's blown it. He admits to lying, cheating, and deceiving his wife. He desperately wants to win her back. Sally says she's here to decide whether the marriage is worth it. She doesn't think so. But she knows she's too angry to think clearly and wants my opinion before signing divorce papers. I gently tell her that advising her about whether to stay with Mark isn't my job. I'll gladly support both of them to make that decision themselves as well as helping them rebuild their marriage if that's what they want.

After their narrative I give them our shortened OHI. I ask the couple how they first met and their first impressions of each other, then what their courtship was like, how they decided to marry, and so on. They both report hot attraction, hotter sex, easy rapport, lots of warmth and affection, and carefully considered commitment. But they also identify some major bumps in the road (more like blockades) early on with Mark's relating to Sally's daughter from her former marriage.

They tell me how these roadblocks became massive conflicts. They had very different approaches to parenting. From his cultural background, Mark believed in holding the reins tight on their daughter, keeping her mostly at home, and during her adolescence scrutinizing every boy she wanted to date. But Sally wanted her daughter to learn by doing and not be hobbled. The daughter had bridled at Mark's fervent control, broken free of his restraints, and run away from home multiple times. Each time, Mark prowled the streets late at night to retrieve her. After they returned, Sally and her daughter would strike an unsteady silent pact against Mark.

Mark reports that he felt ganged up on and excluded. In response, he retreated to the gym, building up his 5'11" body into one nearly as wide. He relates that he loves the gym: the peace, the single-minded focus, the blocking out of home life disharmony, and the brotherhood with his fellow bodybuilders.

Meanwhile, Sally sulked at home alone. Mark's gym time eventually extended from two hours to three and then four. He routinely returned home late, only to be accosted by Sally's wrath—long screaming bouts of contempt and criticism. He flooded physiologically and withdrew when she attacked. In calmer moments, he repeatedly asked Sally what she wanted. Once she spit out, "What do you care?" There were no calm conversations to be had. Mark dug in deeper, retreating from conversation altogether.

Eventually for Mark, loneliness grabbed hold and wouldn't let go. He was reminded of his first days in this country after immigrating. One afternoon thanks to the advent of e-mail, he reconnected with some long lost colleagues. They were scattered around the country now, each with a wife and kids, but they were hungry to once again meet up. They planned a four-day holiday in Las Vegas, just the men without their wives. Play time. Prostitutes were solicited, and the fun was boundless. Another meeting was scheduled. And another. And so it went. Soon, wherever Mark needed to travel for business, call girls were at the ready. In Caracas one especially grabbed his heart. Then there were repeated trips to Caracas. Meanwhile, Sally's daughter, now fully grown, moved out.

Sally's private investigator has fleshed out Mark's story with texts and photos. Mark is now telling the truth about his wanderings, but this is too little too late. A month ago Sally moved out of their home. She has met with an attorney and has already had divorce papers drawn up. On the surface it looks hopeless. Except here they sit, in a therapy office, not a lawyer's.

After they finish their story, we move on. I want to see what conflict management skills this couple has now. Following some words of transition, I ask them if they would be willing to discuss a problem for 10 minutes. Any problem will do. I explain to them that I know it will be difficult to talk in front of me like they do at home, but to please try anyway. I won't be intervening, so I can see at this point how they do on their own. I'll be like a fly on the wall and quietly watch. Witnessing their discussion will help me to discern where they need help and what interventions might work best for them.

For most therapists, this is like having your tooth pulled without anesthesia and remaining silent. Nonetheless, I know it will be useful in my getting to see where this couple gets stuck. It will be like an X-ray where I see which bones are broken and what needs resetting. They warily engage. At various points they pull on me to be judge and jury. Each time I look down at my notes and gesture for them to continue.

I know their interactions are less intense here than at home. Nonetheless their dialogue exposes clear deficits in their conflict management skills. She criticizes, he goes defensive, she ups the ante with well-aimed contemptuous remarks, and he gets flooded. The pulse oximeter on his finger pings steadily as his pulse elevates above the alarm threshold of 100 beats per minute. He shuts down and stonewalls. All Four Horsemen of the Apocalypse (criticism, contempt, defensiveness, and stonewalling), our biggest predictors of relationship demise, stampede over their relationship in 10 minutes flat. Clearly these folks need a new conflict management blueprint in order to resolve issues in a caring manner.

After their 10 minutes are up, we debrief. I thank them, telling them their conversation has shown me where and how they are challenged. I reassure them that even with the pain they're in, I believe they can resurrect their marriage if they want to and they work at it. Marriage #1 may have burnt to the ground, but we may be able to erect marriage #2, this time with bricks and mortar that aren't so easily destroyed. They agree to return next week.

In-between this session and the next one, which will be divided into two individual meetings, I ask Mark and Sally to fill out and mail me a packet of questionnaires. The packet includes our Sound Relationship House questionnaires plus others that examine past incidents of domestic violence, individual symptoms of psychopathology, signs of addiction, marital satisfaction ratings, and so on. A few days later, I receive their packets. The scores portray a landscape of tremendous pain and loneliness. They both report feeling criticized and attacked. They are both in the negative perspective. Mark still responds with "yes" on items about feeling fondness and admiration, but Sally's answers yell out a resounding "no." Both partners feel devalued and unappreciated by one another; both complain of feeling rejected; both feel demeaned and unheard during any discussion; and both have no idea who their partner really is. Neither partner trusts the other, and their marital commitment has evaporated.

On the surface, Mark has shredded Sally's trust with his affairs, and Sally has destroyed Mark's trust by hiring someone to spy on him. But the break in their trust runs deeper. For years neither partner has listened to the other nor responded to the other's needs. Instead, they have coexisted like strangers who share four walls but have even more walls between them. Still, a spark remains, even if in distant memory. In their OHI they have shared stories with me of past love: romantic escapes, laughing at zany movies, trolling beaches for shells, swimming in a moonlit sea, and bathing beneath a Mexican sun. These are embers they remember. Can they be breathed into renewed romance?

Their assessment proves fruitful. It is clear that over time, the way they discuss problems has dynamited their Sound Relationship House down to the foundations, destroying one pillar after another. Gradually the whole structure has weakened into a shaky skeleton of what their relationship once was. Mark's affairs have collapsed the last remaining support walls of trust and commitment, bringing their relationship house down in shambles.

There is much to repair: How hurt and betrayed Sally feels, how her trust has been shattered, and how she no longer knows who her husband is nor whether he's capable of commitment. After Mark answers Sally's questions about the affairs and atones for them, which may take a long time, the whole relationship needs rebuilding. They need to find new ways of turning towards one another rather than away or against each other's bids for connection. They need to replace their old pattern of lacerating each other during conflict with new habits of gently raising and listening to complaints. They need to learn how to describe their own feelings and points of view rather than pointedly describing their partner's flaws.

Although we've got a good roadmap now for what's needed, it doesn't guarantee success for this couple. Up ahead there may still be unforeseen land mines that need dismantling. But with careful assessment and focused interventions, we've got a better chance of rebuilding new foundations and erecting a new stable and strong relationship house.

Let's return to my initial stereotypes about this couple. If I had assumed they were true and immediately intervened without assessing the relationship, I would have alienated Mark in a heartbeat by neglecting his side of things. I would have taken him to be an immoral man who ruined the relationship rather than someone who was deeply hurt by Sally's years of contempt. Intervention would have failed, and the marriage along with it. But with assessment, both partners' contributions to the collapse of their marriage could come into sharp focus, and along with that, a much better plan for recovery.

Remember that average of six years' waiting time before seeking help? Most likely two more weeks of waiting while assessment is conducted won't hinder Mark and Sally's progress. We believe that those sessions of assessment can make a huge difference between groping in the dark, heading nowhere fast, and following a clear roadmap towards relationship recovery.

Bringing It Into Practice

- Conduct a thorough assessment first before beginning intervention.
- Include in the assessment a history of the relationship.
- Measure heart rate while the couple discusses a conflict
- Ask each partner to fill out questionnaires about the couple's friendship, intimacy, conflict management and shared values.
- Choose therapeutic interventions that are based on assessment results.

THE THIRD PRINCIPLE

Understand Each Partner's Inner World

Assessment is complicated. First we have to untangle the frayed threads "in the between," as Martin Buber says, the spun cloth that stretches between two partners. But there's more. We also need to peer within those drawn faces and hear their unspoken words, echoes of past trauma, fears lying in hiding, and yearnings disguised as criticism. These facets are tough to see, let alone understand, without walking first through each partner's early years. This is where individual assessment comes in. Following the first session where the couple has exposed the jagged edges between them, we still need to understand more about how those tangled threads were spun and why they're so fragile.

This brings us to our third principle for effective couples therapy: Understand each partner's inner world.

Then we have the question: What do we need to learn about each partner to best help them? Some questions may lean on our theoretical orientation for individual psychotherapy. For example, say I'm a psychoanalyst. I may tune in to childhood history and hints of transference in the relationship with the other partner and the one with me. If I'm a cognitive therapist, I may inquire about thoughts and beliefs regarding the other partner, the outer world, and self-perception. If I'm a Gestalt therapist, I may only check into the person's experience of the here-and-now.

John and I have found that glancing into each partner's family history is crucial. Early familial connections shape our expectations for the future. If our childhood dinner times were icy with silence, we may only find comfort with partners where little is said and much is read. But if we've come up with noisy dinners crowded with rowdy siblings and parents all clamoring at once, we'll probably think nothing of raucous arguments littered with interruptions.

The movie, *Annie Hall* provides a great example. Woody Allen's character goes to eat with Annie Hall's family. Around their exquisitely set dining table Annie's family members lift and lower their forks in absolute silence. As voyeurs we get that any words aired better be carefully weighed and measured first. Then we shift to Woody's house which happens to sit beneath the Coney Island roller coaster. As the whole place shakes with every car rumbling overhead, his family shoves and yells over one other with perfect comfort. What a contrast!

Then again, partners may not seek the relationship climate they grew up in as much as its opposite. In either case, early life may push partners either forward or backward along the same rutted road. For us to catch even a glimpse of their inner world, we need to learn about their early lives at home. With each partner solo, the following may be helpful questions to ask:

- What was your family like growing up?
- Who raised you and what were your relationships like with them?
- Did you have siblings, and if so, how did you relate to them?
- How did your parents or caregivers relate to one another when you were young? Are they still together, and if not, how old were you when they separated? If they separated or divorced, what effect did that have on you?
- Who comforted you when you were distressed?
- Did anyone in your family use alcohol or drugs? Do you think it was a problem for that person, or for others in the family? What effect do you think it had on you?
- How was discipline handled at home? (This gets at the possibility of physical abuse. If spanking or corporal punishment is mentioned, follow up with more detailed questions about how and by whom the punishment was delivered, and how frequently it occurred.)

Next, we delicately peer into sexual abuse and other traumas during childhood. Because we want to foster feeling safe, if there has been sexual abuse, we don't want partners to feel pressured in any way to expose what they don't want to disclose. Otherwise, we will inadvertently reenact the abuse by violating the person's boundaries and privacy. I like to start off by saying, "I'd like to ask you some more difficult questions now. Will you please let me know if they make you uncomfortable? Because if they do, we will just move on. I know it's hard to talk to someone you've just met, and I want to respect your privacy."

- Other than spankings or other punishment (if there was any), did you ever experience unwanted touch growing up? If so, what kind of touch? Would you tell me whatever you're comfortable sharing about it?
- Have you sought treatment to help you with any aftereffects of your abuse? How was it helpful or not helpful for you?

Taken together these inquiries weave a valuable story, but there still may be holes to fill in. Take, for example, a couple with severe domestic violence. If the couple is seen together, the abused partner may stifle her stories; if she doesn't, she could pay afterward with a brutal beating. If a wife has a secret lover stashed away, she might keep the affair tucked back in shadow as long as her husband shares the therapy room couch with her. In fact, all kinds of secrets might hover unseen: addictions, gambling habits, credit card debts, ugly past traumas, and more. We need to mine for these underground nuggets as well.

Before listing additional questions for our individual interviews, let's discuss domestic violence first.

From Chapter 2, you may recall that John and his colleague, Neil Jacobson, conducted a nine-year research study on domestically violent couples. They described their research and findings in the book, *When Men Batter Women* (Jacobson & Gottman 1998). Like other researchers, they found that there are two types of domestic violence (DV), characterological DV and situational DV. In characterological DV there is a clear perpetrator (in heterosexual couples, usually the man) and clear victim. Characterological perpetrators use their muscles for control and intimidation. They run from responsibility for the violence and instead point their finger at the victim. Nothing the victim does can control or stop the violence. Characterological DV perpetrators may use weapons against their victims, but whether by blow or weapon, the violence may cause serious injury or even death.

John and Jacobson discovered there are two types of characterological DV perpetrators. They called them "pitbulls" and "cobras." Pitbulls are jealous, possessive, and domineering, clenching hold of their victims tenaciously and not letting go. They socially isolate their victims, use threats to intimidate them, and deny all culpability. As they escalate towards violence, their heart rates skyrocket, too. On the other hand, cobras *look like* their heart rates are rising, but physiological measurements reveal that in reality their heart rates are dropping just before they explode. It is all an act. They are also the most terrifying, as their strikes are unpredictable. They aren't particularly possessive but want to ensure the power in the relationship is all theirs; they are provocative and belligerent. They reminded us of cobras because of this fact: A real-life cobra will gently sway back and forth to a flute player's music, and as long as he sways there's no danger. It's when he stops swaying and stills himself that a strike is imminent. Likewise, our DV cobras would still their heads for several moments, then out of nowhere jerk their heads towards the victim and glare as they yelled abuse. On our videotapes we could see the victims' eyes open wide with fear whenever that head stilling took place. They knew what could be coming.

Couples with situational DV look very different. Their violence results from fights in which the Four Horsemen run amok and partners become physiologically flooded. In these fights, both partners are often violent, but the violence is usually minor and does not cause injury. Much to my feminist dismay, Donald Dutton's (1995) book, *The Domestic Assault of Women* reported that in 71% of the heterosexual situational DV fights, it was the woman who threw the first blow. An important distinction between characterological DV couples and their situational DV counterparts is that situational violent partners take full responsibility for their violence and feel deep remorse about it. They will do just about anything to change it. Characterological DV perpetrators have no such guilt or wish to change.

John and I found that our program, Couples Together Against Violence, succeeded in eliminating domestic violence and powerfully improved conflict management in couples with situational DV. As a result, we believe that couples with situational DV can be treated. We know that our point of view strongly differs from that of many clinicians. For that matter, as of this writing, in 31 states couples treatment for any kind of domestic violence is forbidden by law or administrative policies. We believe that these laws are generally a good thing, but one word is missing from their text: "characterological." The laws were written in response to the 20% of women in DV relationships who land in women's shelters. Unlike women with situational DV, these are the victims of characterological DV and life-threatening battery. At long last, victims in these relationships can win protection by law.

On the other hand, it seems wrong to deny couples treatment to those who are not risking injury, who take responsibility for their violence, and who desperately want to change, especially when good research demonstrates that these couples can and do change with the right treatment.

The questions we list below explore whether DV exists in a couple's relationship, and whether the violence is situational or characterological. If there appears to be any possibility of DV judging from the initial conjoint interview, we make it a point to interview who we think the victim is first. That way, if it turns out there is characterological DV, the individual interview with the perpetrator will be handled differently. In most cases, questions about DV with the perpetrator will be avoided altogether to prevent the perpetrator from knowing the victim has been asked the same questions, which could then put her at risk. Characterological DV is a game changer, of course. The therapist's goal will be to help the victim get to safety while telling the perpetrator that at this point, couples therapy is premature or not advised. Individual therapy instead can be recommended for one or both partners.

The next series of questions can be introduced with a statement like this:

"Now I'd like to ask you a standard group of questions that we ask all of our couples."

- Has there been any unwanted touch between you and your partner? (If the partner answers, "yes," follow up with the remaining questions. If the partner seems very uncomfortable with the question, tell the person that if there is any violence and the person is afraid to talk about it for fear of the other partner's reprisal, you will take great care to NOT let the other partner know about these questions or this person's answers, as you want to protect this person's safety. Then see if this person is willing to continue with the following questions.)

- If so, what kind of touch? (Check on slaps, hits with fist, palm or back of hand, kicks, punches, and so on.)
- How often do these episodes happen? What starts them? When was the most recent one?
- Have you ever suffered bruises after one of these episodes? How about cuts, sprains, broken bones? Have you ever needed to seek medical treatment? Did you actually seek the treatment?
- Are you afraid of your partner?
- Have you talked about these episodes with your partner? How does your partner respond? Does your partner take any responsibility for these episodes or does he or she blame you for them?
- Have you ever thought you should leave in order to protect your own safety or that of your children? Have you ever thought about going or have you actually gone to a battered victims' shelter?
- Has your partner ever tried to force you to have sex? Can you tell me what happened?

Answers that indicate severe violence, past injuries, wishes to leave, no responsibility taken by the perpetrator, and fear of the perpetrator all indicate likely characterological DV. Minor DV with no injuries plus the violent partner's guilt and remorse, no fear of the violent partner, and a strong desire to change indicate situational DV.

Let's move on now to questions about affairs. It's important to note that in Gottman Couples Therapy, we encourage clinicians to include in their professional disclosure a statement that they will not keep secret from one partner anything the other partner describes if it is relevant to the therapy. We believe that therapy can only work if it is rooted in truth. Thus, there can be no secrets held between the therapist and one partner while the other partner is kept in the dark (with the exception of cases with characterological DV as just described). A dynamic like this creates an unhealthy collusion. It pits the therapist and one partner against the other partner and sabotages treatment. However, we know that not all therapists believe in this policy. It is up to your discretion.

Before raising the next set of questions, we gently remind partners of our "no secrets" policy. Then we ask the following:

- Have you ever had one or more affairs during this relationship? If so, can you tell me about it (them)?
- Are you having an affair now? (If the answer is "yes" continue with the next questions.)
- How long has it been going on? How did it begin?
- What are your feelings about him or her?
- Have you told your partner about the affair?

At this point, we inform the partner that couples therapy cannot succeed unless the affair ends and it is disclosed to the other partner. We explain: With one foot in each relationship, the partner cannot fully stand in either one. Therapy takes each partner's dedication to the couple's work. A split allegiance between mate and affair partner will compromise the therapy, wasting the couple's time, energy, and resources. If the partner is unwilling to give up the affair, we regretfully say we can't work with the couple. However, if this partner wishes one or two individual sessions to help decide about ending the affair, we will agree to do those or make a referral to someone else.

If the partner has ended the affair but refuses to disclose it to the other partner, again we offer individual help rather than couples work. We often say we've never met anyone who isn't quaking in their boots at the thought of revealing an affair. Everyone assumes disclosure will drown the relationship as surely as an iceberg will sink the *Titanic*. But we give reassurance: As much as confessing the affair will set off a tidal wave, we've seen many relationships not only survive the telling but thrive following the relationship's rebuilding. True, that first wave destroys the illusion that all is well. Every level of the Sound Relationship House collapses as the walls of trust and commitment come tumbling down. But it's likely those walls were eroding anyway. This partner needed to reach out to another, and they both want therapy. Once the terra firma of truth is reached, trust can be slowly rebuilt along with a more enduring relationship. At this point I like to tell the story of a couple John and I treated where one partner had 57 affairs over the course of 12 years. So loud were his lies that they deafened his wife. She was out the door with kids in tow. After many, many tears and no guarantees, they agreed to rebuild. And rebuild they did. They called it their Marriage #2.

Of course, gentle persuasion may fail. The partner may still resist breathing a word about the affair to the other partner. In that case, we regretfully say we cannot work with the couple. If requested, we may tell the other partner that as it turns out, we are not a good fit for them. If they wish another referral, we can make one.

The last questions in our interview zero in on drug and alcohol use. We ask both partners to detail what they consume, how frequently, and how much. We also track if the amounts have grown over time and the effects of their use. In addition we ask each person about the habits of their partner. This enables us to compare self-report with partners' perceptions. If one partner sees the other using much more than that partner acknowledges, we've got denial operating, the red flag of addiction. We will need to address how addiction contaminates connection between partners and offer treatment options. Here are helpful questions to ask:

- Do you take prescribed medication(s)? Can you list which ones and their dosages? For what conditions are you taking each one? Who is the doctor prescribing them for you? (At this point, we ask the individual to give us written consent to consult with the doctor about their treatment.)
- Do you drink alcohol? If so, how many times a week do you drink?
- On average, how many drinks do you consume at one time?
- What is your drink of choice?
- Do you use any recreational drugs? Which ones?
- How often do you use these drugs? How much at one time?
- Has anyone around you expressed concern about your alcohol or drug use? If so, what are their concerns?
- Do you think your usage is impacting your social life? Your work life? Your family life? How so?
- Do you think your alcohol or drug use is a problem for you? If yes, have you tried getting treatment? What was the

outcome of your treatment? Would you consider getting an evaluation for treatment?

- Do you consume caffeine? In what form? How many cups or drinks a day? (If more than three, check on their nightly hours and quality of sleep.)

We finish up the interview with questions arising from any hints of a mental disorder or behavioral abnormalities. We check for underlying symptoms of depression, posttraumatic stress disorder, bipolar disorder, personality disorder, behavioral addiction, or other conditions that may be troubling each partner. If we find evidence of any, we discuss options for evaluation and treatment.

I like to close my interview by asking the partner if he or she has any questions for me before we stop for the day. This balances the scales a bit and illustrates that their questions, concerns, and comments about the work are fine and I welcome them. Then we're done.

Let's look at a case study where the individual interview was crucial for assessment and treatment.

In our first meeting, Robert and Mattie showed up promptly, looking immaculate but worn out. He wore a day or two of stubble, a white shirt, perfectly pressed jeans, and a blue sweater. She had on a narrow leather skirt, scarlet silk top, paisley tights, and tall black boots. They were both tan, but underneath there was a strained pallor. They told me how their relationship plummeted once their child was born. That was a year and a half ago. They had been fighting ever since.

After our first session together, I met with each partner individually. Robert was president of his own company. He had built it straight out of high school. He glowed with pride as he described his success. He'd obviously polished his image to impress. Yet there was a hint of insecurity here, a need to please that didn't fit with the nonchalance he tried to project. His manners were too studied, his speech too wordy, his legs too tightly crossed. There were cracks in his veneer.

I asked him about his childhood. What were his relationships like with his dad, mom, and two brothers? If he could use one word to describe each, what word would he choose? For Dad, "tough." For Mom, "vacant." For his older brother, "bad-ass." And for the younger brother, "crushed." Not the perfect family.

Born into a rich aristocratic bloodline, Robert had been raised in Belgium. His father bore some sort of title. Their home was one of those Downton Abbey hulking estates, complete with black-capped servants. He hated it. There were scores of cold stone rooms, long dim hallways, and ancient creaky furniture for "look, don't touch." As a youngster he had playfully cavorted on one of the guest beds, but down it came, a sixteenth-century antique, now broken and ruined. The nanny walloped him for that one. Robert ran crying to his dad and told him what she'd done. Cool and cruel, Dad's response was to hit him harder, claiming a woman wasn't strong enough to do him justice. Meanwhile, Mother drank. Very quietly. Very secretly. It was easy given how many rooms she could hide in.

His brothers tried to survive, each in his own way. The eldest stole money from Mom, commandeered a motorcycle, and left home at 15. Learning later that he had headed to Mexico, the Federales were summoned. They caught up with him and dragged him onto a jet back to Belgium. He left again at 17, and this time the parents let him go and cut him off. He was as good as dead. Robert hadn't seen him since. Meanwhile his younger brother stayed home, started sneaking drinks young, cowered when Father was near, and cloistered himself in his room.

Robert figured he was lucky when his parents shipped him off to a high-class boarding school in South America. Great, an ocean away from home. But nothing got easier. One Wednesday night after class, a teacher invited him home, offered him scotch, and several drinks later added his penis to the mix. The teacher threatened to fail him if he breathed a word of it. He was told he must return weekly. Thereafter, while his dormmates whooped and watched soccer, Robert's Wednesday nights at the teacher's house became a nightmare. Finally summer break arrived. Should he tell his parents? But that would mean returning to the fold and transferring to a school near home. Forced to choose between one hell and another, he opted to stay mum and go back to school. Four years later he emerged bitter, ferociously determined, ambitious, and traumatized. With money from his grandmother, he grabbed hold of the reins of a small company and within 10 years expanded it internationally. Opening headquarters in the United States was his goal. By 28, he'd done it.

Mattie's childhood read like a Dickens novel transplanted to Iowa. She grew up on the crooked porch of a cramped Midwestern hovel. Her father was stone deaf, the result of manning heavy artillery in World War II. After the war he had migrated back home and married Mattie's mother, his high school sweetheart. While he fought Germans, she had become a dance teacher. But once they married Dad insisted she quit, enforcing his reign with his fists. Two years later, Mattie was born. She grew up learning sign language.

The family lived on Dad's disability benefits, barely enough to cover costs. As Mattie grew older, she sparked with artistic talent plus gumption. The latter, Dad didn't like. Out of the blue as with Mom, he would hit Mattie, too. His blows were like blocks of iron that sent her careening off the porch. Terrified by now, Mom would look away and stay silent. Mattie would shakily rise, brush herself off, and retreat upstairs. There she would sit and stare out the window at the snow swirling into four-foot drifts, wishing she could fall sleep inside one, gone but safe. As we talked she mentioned in passing that many of her paintings featured swirls of white with lost figures within them.

Intervention began in earnest after their assessment and goal-setting. Over the course of their first 10 sessions they worked hard to learn new conflict management skills.

Then came our 11th meeting. As I opened my door, they stomped into my room. Robert looked particularly vexed. Their conflict? How to decorate the Christmas tree. Robert demanded pure white candle-style lights; Mattie begged for lava lamps. Since I only celebrated Hanukkah, I didn't grasp what the fuss was about. And what were lava lamps anyway? There had to be more to this conflict than met the eye. I suggested using the Dream-Within-Conflict exercise to discuss the issue. (We'll go into more detail about this exercise in a later chapter.)

In this exercise, one partner is the speaker and one is the listener. The speaker's job is to describe his or her point of view and answer questions posed by the listener. The listener's job is to simply read aloud a list of questions, one by one, and listen to the speaker's answers. John and I had designed this exercise together during one particularly inspired and caffeinated late-night work session. The questions dip into beliefs, childhood history, ideal dreams, and existential meanings that underlie the speaker's position on the issue being discussed. The listener is cautioned to not bring up his or her own point of view until the roles are reversed and it's his or her turn to be the new speaker.

Mattie began as the speaker. She waxed poetic about lava lamps, describing how she would watch the bubbles drifting upward and feel herself unfettered and free as if she, too, was a bubble floating skyward above the snowy rooftops outside.

Robert asked the next question down the list, "Is there a story or some childhood history that relates to your position on this issue?"

"Well...." . . ." She paused. "I guess Christmas was peaceful. Unusually so."

Here was a hint of Mattie's individual session and her description of the war zone that was home.

"May I interrupt for a moment?" I asked.

"Sure."

"Mattie, does Robert know how bad things were in your home the rest of the time?"

"Probably not."

"How about telling him about that?"

"Well . . ."

She did, detailing the blows, the pain, a broken wrist, the terror, and the burning rage inside, how unpredictable her father was, and the injustice of it all.

I added, "So Christmas was like a demilitarized zone in time, when your home was safe, there were no fights, and everyone could let down and relax a little."

"Yes, from 6 p.m. Christmas eve to midnight on Christmas, we actually loved each other. That's it. Lava lamps mean love to me. And peace." She looked sad.

"Oh, I see." Robert softly said.

After more questions and exploration, they traded roles. It was Robert's turn to be the speaker.

Mattie asked, "So what are your beliefs about this issue?"

Robert replied, "White candle lights are pure, beautiful, clean. They reveal the purity of God."

Then that key question again: "Is there some childhood history related to your position on this issue?"

"Umm. In high school, coming home for Christmas was a good time. Everyone was nicer. It was pure. Kind of innocent somehow."

(Pure, clean, innocent? Bells rang from his individual session.)

I whispered to Mattie, "Try asking him what was so meaningful about how 'pure' those times were. What does he mean by 'pure'?"

She did.

His dark eyes dropped to the carpet, then fixed on me.

"I've never told her," he muttered under his breath.

"Told me what?" She looked startled.

I nodded. "It's okay. It might help if she knew."

"But what if it makes things worse?"

"I don't think it will, but it's up to you. It's totally your choice. You don't have to do anything you don't want to do."

Mattie said, "Oh come on. Just tell me. I won't bite."

Haltingly at first, he slowly uttered his story, again his gaze glued to the carpet as he described his high school Wednesday nights.

Her eyes grew round and moist. "Oh, Robert, honey, why didn't you ever tell me?"

"Too ashamed. I thought you'd hate me. Or call me a fag."

"Never, never, never. For God's sake, you were just a child!"

She grabbed his hand and pulled him towards her.

For both Robert and Mattie, secret stories from childhood lay buried beneath their conflicted Christmas tree visions. White candlelight for Robert transported him back to the innocence he had once possessed but later lost. Their lovely glow obscured the shadows that tainted his childhood. Likewise for Mattie, the bubbling beauty of lava lamps returned her to those precious moments when her family had coexisted in peace. Without the individual sessions and the gold they yielded, the revelations they shared with another might never have seen the light of day. And without them, their conversation might have ended where it began, in a well-defended standoff.

Thirty minutes later Robert and Mattie had the whole issue solved. The candlelights would be attached to one electrical cord and the lava lamps to another. For half the day they would plug in one cord and for the second half, the other, except when their toddler was up and in the living room when they would plug in both: a grand display.

Bringing It Into Practice

- Use individual interviews to begin building a therapeutic alliance.
- Maintain a "no secrets" policy to avoid colluding with one partner against the other.
- Couples therapy should only proceed if an extra-marital affair has ended.
- If domestic violence is suspected, first interview the partner you think is the victim and find out if the violence is situational or characterological.
- Do not do couples therapy if there is characterological domestic violence. Help the victim to create a safety plan.
- Inquire about drug and/or alcohol use.
- Ask about each partner's childhood and earlier significant relationships.

THE FOURTH PRINCIPLE
Map Your Treatment Route

So far we've discussed the face-to-face elements of assessment: a series of interviews conducted with the couple seen together and separately. Between conjoint and individual sessions, we also ask partners to privately fill out a packet of questionnaires.

The packet resembles a jeweler's looking glass. Peering through its lens, we see multiple facets of the relationship. Some are pure, some are damaged, telling us what not to touch and where to make repairs.

The packet contains scales we developed and tested for examining each level of the Sound Relationship House, plus questionnaires that alert us to the presence of domestic violence and emotional abuse. We also include inventories created by other scientists to explore everything from overall relationship satisfaction to individual psychopathology.

The first two questionnaires in the packet estimate how well the relationship is doing overall. The Locke-Wallace Relationship

Adjustment Test measures relative satisfaction and happiness; the Weiss-Cerretto Relationship Status Inventory counts the steps partners have taken towards divorce. Taken together, these give us valuable information, especially when we see that one partner is already interviewing lawyers while the other seems blissfully unaware and happy.

Next come the Sound Relationship House questionnaires. When we started in the lab, each scale was 20–30 items long. Thankfully, John has performed recent item-analysis work to reduce each one to five items, with each item packing powerful revelation.

These scales measure partners' perception of every brick in their Sound Relationship House, including love maps, fondness and admiration, turning towards, the negative perspective, the Four Horsemen, harsh start-up, repair attempts, gridlocked conflict, flooding, compromise, and symbols, roles, goals, and rituals of shared meaning. Additional scales examine emotional disengagement and loneliness, sex, romance and passion, trust, and commitment. A different kind of scale invites comments about how partners are handling particular issues like financial matters, in-laws, work, and external stress.

We've added questionnaires to uncover abuse, both emotional and physical. Our scales called "Acts of Physical Aggression," "Control," and "Fear" not only look for violence but also pinpoint whether the violence is situational or characterological. As we described, this is crucial to know. If there's evidence of characterological violence, couples therapy may put the victim at grave risk and thus is contraindicated.

Finally, we look for signs of individual psychopathology using the 90-item Symptom Check List (SCL-90) and a Suicide Potential Scale. Drug and alcohol problems are weighed with the CAGE Questionnaire and the Brief Michigan Alcohol Screening Test. We use these scales to signal when individual treatment may be needed.

At first glance, the questionnaire packet is thick and daunting. At every one of our trainings, a clinician invariably asks, "Do we have to give our clients all of these?"

Yes, and here's why: First, the information they give us is invaluable. We learn much more about each partner's disgruntlement than a few hours of interview can provide. Second, we've found that people actually like to take these questionnaires. They arouse the same curiosity that drives people to fill out magazine quizzes about romance, love, and personality. People are desperate to know where they stand. When people are in the middle of flagging relationships, it can feel like they're lost in a white-out. They can't see what's up, what's down, what's sideways. Without bearings, they can't find their way home. Invariably couples have told us these questionnaires help them see their relationship strengths and not just the challenges. The overlook lifts them above the fog and gives them hope.

Once we have scored the questionnaires, we integrate the data with the results of our interviews to map out the couple's strengths and challenges and plot their course for treatment. With Greendorfer's admonition about driving without planning in mind, this analysis gives our fourth principle for successful couples therapy: Map your treatment route.

Assessment maps our coordinates. We described the assessment methods we prefer because they are all based on careful research with established reliability and validity. Recently we transferred our full questionnaire packet to an Internet site. Clinicians can send their couples to the site to take the questionnaires individually. After both partners complete them, the clinician automatically receives each partner's scores plus detailed recommendations for treatment based on those scores. (See http://www.Gottman.com for further information.)

Of course we understand that you may conduct couples therapy using a different orientation. Your analyses may spring from a different model for what couples need to fare well and how to help them get there. Whatever system you use, we simply hope it includes assessment. If it does, you can take some reassurance that your interventions won't waste the couple's time and resources or yours. In other words, your help can target the couple's problems areas rather than ones where the couple is doing just fine.

We like to analyze our data by using our Clinician's Checklist for Couple Assessment. The checklist is based on the SRH theory and our model for assessment and treatment. It lists the most important factors we need to map out treatment goals. By scouring scores and interview data we check off the appropriate boxes on our list. The list provides both diagnosis and recommendations for specific treatment goals we should pursue. We've supplied the Checklist for you here.

CLINICIAN'S CHECKLIST FOR RELATIONSHIP ASSESSMENT

This checklist provides a way to organize and summarize your assessment of a couple's relationship. Keep in mind the Sound Relationship House as you consider these questions.

- ☐ **CHAOS?**

- ☐ **ARE THERE FUNDAMENTAL MISMATCHES?**

- ☐ **BETRAYALS?**

- ☐ **OVERALL, WHERE ARE THEY EACH IN THE RELATIONSHIP?**

- ☐ **IS COUPLES THERAPY CONTRAINDICATED?**

- ☐ **THE COUPLE FRIENDSHIP**

  — The Fondness and Admiration system

  — Love Maps

  — Signs of emotional disengagement

  — Stresses

  — Fun

  — Loneliness

  — Parallel lives

☐ **SENTIMENT OVERRIDES**

— How humor and anger get responded to

— Ability to self-soothe

— Ability to soothe partner

☐ **REGULATING CONFLICT**

— Stonewalling or other disengagement

— Softened or Harsh Startup

— Compromise

— Dialogue about perpetual problems

☐ **GENDER ISSUES**

☐ **MESHING LIFE DREAMS AND CREATING SHARED SYMBOLIC MEANING**

☐ **PSYCHOPATHOLOGY**

☐ **PAST TRAUMA**

☐ **POTENTIAL RESISTANCES**

☐ **OVERALL PROGRESS TOWARDS BEING ABLE TO CREATE OR MAINTAIN SHARED MEANING SYSTEM**

Let's review. When couples come to us for help, here's what we think they need the most from us: (1) our knowledge of what a healthy relationship looks like; (2) our analyses of what each partner contributes to the relationship's dynamics; (3) our understanding of each partner's inner world; (4) our pinpointing what changes the couple needs to make to achieve a healthier and more satisfying relationship; and (5) our creative interventions that can move them from a relationship house built of straw to one that is healthier, happier, and rock-solid.

Let's consider an illustration. Bill and Cindy entered therapy as a last-ditch effort before waving the white flag of defeat and divorcing. They had both consulted attorneys a month ago. When they took an honest look at their 12- and 13-year-old daughters who were flourishing in their currently intact family, they had stopped midstream and called me instead.

Bill labeled himself a "supreme tech geek" whose upbringing was "extremely weird." His dad was an electrical engineer and "a social moron" who often embarrassed Bill by acting bizarrely. Void of emotion, Bill saw him as a robot cursed with crossed wires. Bill's two younger sisters shunned Dad like the plague. When adults, they had both accused him of molesting them as kids, a charge he loudly denied.

Bill's mother had donned a nun's black habit at age 16, but 14 years later Bill's father convinced her to cast celibacy aside and marry him. Their union was a disaster except for the three kids they conceived. For many years they slept in separate rooms and rarely talked. Their icy house was like a tomb. Bill escaped to the streets, wildly biking with his neighborhood buddies whenever he could.

An awful day came after Bill turned 12. His father proclaimed they were joining four other families to form a faith-based farming commune. Bill was wrenched away from his beloved friends and thrust into Yehupetz (Yiddish for the middle of nowhere). For the next three years he was arm-twisted into sitting in a barren, one-room, all-grade schoolhouse where his only ally was another disgruntled teen. With no knowledge of farming to speak of, the commune hung on by the skin of its teeth, nearly starving every winter. Bill thought he was going to go crazy. In desperation, he finally convinced his parents to send him back to his hometown where he could live with the family of an old friend and attend a decent school.

Gloriously happy now, he steamrolled from there to a top-notch college, worked his tail off, and graduated summa cum laude. A week after graduating, a high-tech company vacuumed him up. There he hunkered down, worked 100 hours a week, and rapidly rose to a high-level position in just five years.

Cindy's story was as rich as Bill's was bleak. She was raised in a large close-knit family in which they did chores together and spent their weekends camping out or going on long, winding country drives. Although her parents rarely expressed affection and emotion openly, Cindy always felt loved and cherished. She later attended a local university, majored in business, and went on to work in marketing for the same company that hired Bill.

They met at a company party. Bill was entranced by Cindy's glittering, vivacious personality—the exact opposite of his. Cindy admired Bill's ethic of hard work and his obvious intellectual brilliance. They dated happily for two years. But when Cindy turned 33, her biological clock boomed like a bass drum. Impatient to "get on with it," she delivered Bill an ultimatum: "Marry me or else." He reverted to logic. She was a reasonably good choice for a wife, right? They had fun, got along fine, and she was pretty, so why not?

Soon after the wedding, Cindy insisted they try to have kids. She was blessed with her mom's fertility. Two daughters popped out in just 23 months. But Bill hadn't reckoned how hard it would be to have two kids in diapers. Sleepless and depressed, he spent even more hours at the office. Cindy quit her job to take on child-care full-time.

Their lives diverged from one to two roads; Bill's road headed for the high peaks while Cindy steamed along on the low road. Bill soon became a company vice president, while Cindy designed their four houses and volunteered in the kids' school. Despite outward appearances, however, all was not well. Sex petered out to a dribble and then to never. Conversation dwindled down to "Did you call the plumber?" Dinner times featured Cindy and the kids amicably chatting while Bill downed his meal and scurried back to his den. Cindy tried over and over to entice Bill into the family mix, but Bill buried himself in paperwork instead. Years flew by. Their impasse soon became impenetrable.

Now, a decade later, they sat wondering whether their marriage could be salvaged. In reviewing what they had told me when together and apart, plus their questionnaire scores, it was clear that whatever dull embers of their marriage remained would take a mighty wind to rekindle. Their questionnaires indicated miles of emotional distance that separated them, compounded by terrible loneliness and confusion. Bitter criticisms had salted their past attempts to resolve their differences, killing off any new growth between them. It had been so long since they'd had conversation, let alone intimacy, that they really didn't know who their partner was anymore.

Facing these two was daunting. It was our third session together. Prior to meeting, I had analyzed how they had interacted during their initial session, what they had told me individually, and how they had answered their questionnaire items. I integrated their data into the Assessment Checklist to help organize my thinking about their treatment. Normally I'm pretty optimistic, but these two left me feeling hopeless. How to set goals for these poor people? In reviewing their case back home, I shook my head.

They had a fundamental mismatch in how they dealt with emotion. Cindy preferred keeping a cheerful, upbeat attitude. She rode through bad times like a barge that cuts through any wave. In contrast Bill was a 12-foot sailboat tossed and tumbled by every storm. Decades ago when he had approached Cindy for support, she always recited the message she had heard all her life: "Cheer up, it's not so bad."

On the friendship levels of their Sound Relationship House, the floors were rotting. Their love maps were out of date by a decade. They hadn't expressed fondness and admiration to each other since their kids were born. And turning towards bids for connection was nonexistent. They had stopped making bids years ago because the bids invariably failed. So little positive energy remained in the relationship that negative sentiment override weighed it down like a truckload of cement.

They had also suffered through many years of conflict. Cindy had reverted to the Four Horsemen to crash through Bill's walls.

Her words had sent Bill running for the hills. He had reached a point where he could smell a conflict coming like a bad snowstorm. Soon he stopped talking to Cindy altogether. It had been years since they had discussed their differences.

Bill and Cindy's connection had unraveled and left little if any threads connecting them. That included updating and sharing their beliefs and values. They had no idea what goals motivated the other or what dreams the other held dear. There was only one life purpose they shared: their children. The kids were their glue. Fortunately, their parenting styles overlapped, but that was the only bridge between them.

I looked over their assessment checklist and sighed.

During moments like these (and over the years there have been many), my saving grace is a fundamental belief: It's not up to us to decide whether we should try to rescue a couple and resurrect their marriage or throw it on the garbage heap. That decision is the couple's to make. All we can do is describe what we see as the truth of their relationship's strengths and weaknesses, lay out as accurately as we can what route might take them from misery to contentment, and then sit back and see what they want to do. Set treatment goals, in other words, but in consideration of what *they* want, not necessarily what we want.

To open up their third session of assessment, I handed Bill and Cindy a picture of the Sound Relationship House with its seven levels clearly labeled. We discussed each level one by one, starting from the bottom and moving up.

"The first level we call, 'Love Maps,'" I said. "This level refers to how well you know the landscape of your partner's inner world. For example, for you, Cindy, it would mean knowing what Bill's needs are or what his current priorities and worries are... or for you, Bill, knowing who Cindy's best friends are, what her favorite book is, what her favorite vacation destination is, and so on. On this level, there's a lot of work that's needed. It appears that you've been like trains traveling down parallel tracks for a long time, beside one another but not intersecting. You've lost touch with one another. It's been so long, you hardly know who your partner is anymore. If you want to work on this marriage, you'll need to work on creating 'Love Maps' of one another by finding out who your partner is here and now, what's important to him or her. It's like surveying your partner's inner landscape. Figuring out what kind of person he or she has evolved to become. I have some tools that can help with this if you decide to go forward with therapy. So far, does what I've just described make sense to you?"

They nodded.

I dreaded explaining the next level.

Fondness and Admiration is the next floor of the Sound Relationship House. This level pertains to not only how much love and admiration you feel for your partner but also how well you express those to one another. Couples who do well in this area are physically affectionate, express daily appreciations for the small things their partners do every day, and often give each other warm compliments. They cherish each other. And they work hard to prioritize time for conversations together and treasure their time for lovemaking."

Cindy burst out, "We suck at that." Bill glanced at her, then away.

I went on. "I'm afraid you're right, Cindy. It looks like you two have grown so distant that you haven't had a real in-depth conversation in years, and no sex to speak of either. Instead, you have filled up your lives with separate interests and activities. Unfortunately there's been no sharing of these, no junctions between you. And that has left a void in place of connection. Now it looks like you are both very lonely in this marriage, although you never speak of it to one another. That's very sad. Neither of you feels cherished nor appreciated by the other. At this point, you may not be sure you still even love your partner. Your lives are full—Bill, with your work colleagues and projects, and Cindy with the kids and your volunteer work—but you're left with nothing to give each other. So now you have a choice. If you choose to work on the marriage, you'll need to cut back on some of those activities to make room for time with each other. That may not feel very good at first. After all, those activities have been filling up the void between you pretty well. And if you cut back on some of them, there's no guarantee that your marriage will grow enough to take their place and fill up the space. You may end up down at the bottom of the chasm again, feeling empty and lonely. But there's also a chance that if you work hard on connecting and loving one another, you may end up with something much better than you'd dreamed of—a marriage that enriches you and gives you joy. It's a gamble, I know. But it's up to you—your choice." I waited for their reply.

Bill looked at Cindy. Cindy looked at Bill. Then they both looked down at their hands, so politely folded in their laps. "I don't know," said Bill. Cindy shrugged. "For the kids' sake, I want to at least try, Bill. I don't want our kids hitting adolescence with a divorce in their wake."

Bill quietly said, “But I’m really lonely. I have been for years. I really don’t know if I want this marriage anymore. I just don’t feel anything.”

Here was a moment of truth. I had a lot of choices at this point. I could jump in with cheerful hope and promises of great exercises that could accomplish miracles and then encourage them to give it a shot. Or I could say, “You’re probably right, Bill. This marriage is dead in the water, doomed—plain and simple. Better that you both move on and look for new partners.” Or I could chide them for even thinking about giving up. “What about those marriage vows you took? Don’t those mean anything to you?”

I did none of the above. Instead I hit the pause button and waited. And waited. A good five minutes passed in rugged silence.

Finally Bill said, “Well, I guess it couldn’t hurt. Might as well try. We’ll see what happens. But I don’t want to try for very long. I’ve already wasted enough time.”

Ouch. But Cindy remained silent.

And that was their decision, in a nutshell.

I went on to describe my findings on the remaining Sound Relationship House levels. They agreed with my findings for each one. On Level 3, Turning Towards, or how well they responded to each other’s bids for connection, the findings were obvious. What bids? There was nothing to respond to, therefore this level needed mountains of work. On Level 4, the Positive or Negative Perspective, or whether they gave their partner the benefit of the doubt most of the time, or perceived negativity every time their partner blinked an eye, the data reflected a resounding “negative.” On Level 5, “Managing Conflict,” or how well they discussed their differences and worked to resolve their problems, the results were a mild "not bad." Although criticism and defensiveness destructively popped up between them now and then, they mostly handled their problems fairly well. However, they had never tackled the deeper differences between them and chose to avoid them instead, which suffocated any chance they had to understand each other better. On the surface, Level 6 or "Honoring Each Other's Dreams," looked pretty good. They had mostly done so but not with intention. Bill's money had allowed Cindy to pursue her passion for home design, and Cindy's penchant for homemaking and parenting had liberated Bill to pursue his work ambitions. They hadn't actively supported each other's life dreams, but due to their own native talents and hard work, they'd created lives that fulfilled them individually although leaving their marriage empty. Finally, we reached Level 7, "Creating Shared Meaning." This level looked at how well they understood each other's beliefs, core values, and goals, and how well they had created together a life of shared meaning and purpose together. On this level they were at best lukewarm. Yes, they had both believed in hard work and had dedicated themselves individually to what gave each of their lives purpose, but the inner gems of their beliefs hadn't been shared with each other. They were more like two people living in parallel, each with his or her life purpose, but with neither person sharing with or supporting the other. Like two apple trees growing side-by-side but with no cross-fertilization.

The path ahead was clear. Work on building friendship. Work on helping these two feel safe enough with each other that they could begin to share their inner worlds with one another. Help them design rituals of connection, that is, predictable, intentional ways to spend time together that could provide them both with comfort and contentment. And if their trust in the relationship grew, eventually tackle those big differences, the gridlocked conflict areas they had swept under the carpet for years—like renegotiating the balance between Bill's work and time spent together as a family.

It remained to be seen how this relationship would fare in the future. But at least we now had a roadmap to follow, one based on careful evaluation of this couple's idiosyncrasies plus the direction in which they needed to travel, so they could hopefully find some light at the end of their long dark tunnel. Together, the three of us shifted into drive and moved forward.

Bringing It Into Practice

- Compile data from assessment interviews and questionnaires.
- Use Clinicians' Assessment Checklist to organize data
- Use the Sound Relationship House to explain assessment findings to the couple.
- Based on the assessment, decide on treatment goals with the couple.

THE FIFTH PRINCIPLE

Soothe Yourself, Then Intervene

It was Tuesday, almost 4 p.m. The most challenging couple of the week was about to arrive. James was a lanky plastic surgeon, 6'4" with the trim body of a cyclist. Dressed in Northwest style, he wore faded jeans, a striped shirt open at the collar, and a salt and pepper mustache. A migrant from New York, he had settled in Seattle 20 years earlier and built a stellar career catering to the wishes of wealthy women who raced to outpace their falling jowls and wrinkled necklines. As it turned out, the good doctor had serviced several of these patients in more ways than one.

Lynette, his wife, had just discovered his backdoor erotic adventures. She was tiny, barely grazing 4'11". A pixie cut red-head, slender, mini-skirted and like lightning plugged in, she was on fire. For six sessions she had launched into enraged tirades at James. Last week, she'd leaped off the couch and screamed, "How could you? You Goddamn bastard! I hate your guts! Did you ever think of me? Did you ever think of our kids? You're a destroyer!

That's what you are! You're Satan!" Given the decibel level of her speech, I was glad my suitemates had headed home for the night.

My 10-minute break ticked by. Dread set up shop in my stomach. This was not going to be fun. In one recent session, Lynette had checked herself from launching upward. She had remained seated. But after the couple left, I found scratch marks made by her fingernails in my new red leather couch. Some couples get very angry.

This pair may typify your worst nightmare: two partners who are so hostile and tormented that they flood with rage in seconds like scalded milk boiling over. In therapy our challenge is to stay calm and gently contain their anger. We have to walk a tightrope between helping them to vent their feelings and stopping any abuse. It takes some skill, but more fundamentally, our ability to stay calm in the face of rage. In effect, with couples like these we are volunteering to leap into a live volcano and ride the lava flow downhill until it eventually cools and settles.

Let's talk about what causes flooding like this in the first place. Flooding is another name for diffuse physiological arousal (DPA), the physical response John and his colleague Robert Levenson discovered in their research when they measured what was happening to some couples as they escalated during quarrels. In the middle of conflict-related discussions, partners who flooded might look slumped, passive, and quiet, but internally their hearts were racing at over 100 beats per minute. Their blood pressure was skyrocketing, their shallow respiration, quickening, and their skin, perspiring. In short, they were being hijacked by cortisol and the adrenaline-fueled fight-or-flight response, a well-evolved reaction to being attacked. Flooding was blocking them from thinking clearly, addressing problems creatively, accessing their empathy and humor, and hearing their partner's words accurately. Flooding was also producing tunnel vision and hearing that mistranslated any messages they perceived into signals of attack.

John and Levenson found that flooded couples could not solve their interpersonal problems. Only after taking a break, calming down, and regaining a normal physiological state could they have a fruitful problem-solving conversation.

Another colleague of John's, Dr. Steve Porges, found in his research that our propensity to flood is also regulated by the tone of our Vagus nerve. The Vagus is the 10th cranial nerve, named so because the Latin word *vagus* means "wanderer." The Vagus nerve travels throughout the body, regulating the systems that help us automatically respond to environmental stimuli. The Vagus serves as a brake on the heart, slowing its pulse rate. If we face an enemy, the firing of the Vagus nerve is inhibited, releasing the brakes so our heart rate can increase in a moment or two. Then our Sympathetic Nervous System signals us to move into full-on fight-or-flight.

Porges found that the tonality of the Vagus varies. Some people possess good Vagal tone. The degree to which they react to an environmental stimulus is reasonably proportional to the intensity of the stimulus. But those with poor Vagal tone overreact to a stimulus. When they feel threatened, their hearts beat out of control like a truck racing downhill, and they take longer to apply the brakes. They are more likely to have big reactions to minor stimuli, and it takes them much longer to calm down afterwards.

Flooding doesn't just plague our clients. It can infect us, too. As our clients escalate, sometimes so do we. We worry, will these people lose control? We have thoughts like, "What will I do if he goes ballistic and starts yelling?" "What will I do if she verbally lunges at him?" "What if their voices get so loud it disturbs my suitemate and his client next door?" We get frightened. Nonetheless, if we want to help our couples, we need to remain calm so we can intervene with the right words at the right moment, a tall order even if we're not flooded. We don't want to jump in too fast before the couple tries their own ways of gentling the conversation. But we should also move in before things get ugly if the couple can't deescalate on their own. Timing is everything. If we're flooded, it's easier for us to blow it, to jump in too soon and do all the soothing for them. Worse, we might inadvertently nail one partner while the other one watches in glee and gloats in victory.

One year, John and I were being filmed as we worked with a couple, Dave and Linda. Their marriage was in shambles. Every time she opened her mouth, razor-sharp criticisms and lots of contempt poured out. We were doing intensive work with the couple, Marathon Therapy, a model where we see couples five to six hours a day for three or four consecutive days. It had been a roller coaster, but we were finally starting to get somewhere. They were calming down their conflict management and understanding more about each other's underlying triggers. Yesterday had been a slog through wet concrete, and this was our last day of the marathon. By now I was feeling pretty ragged. Today we would focus on the positive side of things.

We asked each partner to review a list of 70 positive personal characteristics and then name several traits they thought their mate possessed. They were also instructed to cite a memory of how their mate had demonstrated each trait. When it was Dave's turn, he described how beautiful Linda was and how much he loved looking at her face. He recalled gazing at her during their last candlelit anniversary dinner. "Oh, that's ridiculous," she replied. "You're such a liar! You were just trying to get in my pants. Ha!"

With that I'd had it. Criticism, again? I could feel the heat rising. In frustration I clapped my hands once, loudly, and exclaimed, "Linda. Stop!"

She looked stunned and maybe a little hurt. Meanwhile, Dave looked surprised. But then he smiled, just a little one—I'm guessing he felt victorious as my frustration boiled over just like his had many times before. Maybe he thought, "You get it now. See how awful she is?"

Immediately, I felt guilty and ashamed. What a lousy therapist I was! Punishing her like a first-grade teacher yells at the class clown. What kind of gentle intervention was that, let alone role modeling for Dave? A good day to switch professions.

In the next moment I realized that Linda's comment was designed to push Dave away. He had gotten too close to her. If she had allowed herself to take in Dave's loving comments, she would feel more open to him, more vulnerable and visible. Because she had been taught she was worthless early on and still believed it, she feared that the closer Dave got the more he would see her faults, what she saw as her unworthiness and ugliness. So with a well-aimed verbal kick, she had shoved him away.

It made me mad. I had seen such lovely progress between them. Why did she have to sabotage it? I wanted control over every word she said. No doubt I was flooded. My heart rate was right up there. How come?

At a deeper level, I had let my own feelings creep in. I'd staked my being a good therapist on the performance of my clients, like a mom who wants her son's high dive to be perfect because his success will mean she's a great mom. Along the same vein Linda's criticism reflected what I worried was my own professional inadequacy. And on top of everything it was all on film. The video camera was like God's eye in the sky judging me. Linda's failure was mine, too.

It all happened in a heartbeat, my own poor Vagally toned one. In an attempt to counteract my authoritarianism with compassion, I reflected how difficult it was for Linda to let in Dave's compliment and why that might be so. I spoke of how much she had been neglected growing up, how her mother's brutal criticisms had left her feeling worthless, how her step-father's beatings had drilled in the same message, and how dangerous it was now to allow anyone to get close, lest they see all that unworthiness in her. In the moment, her criticism of Dave had made perfect sense. It shoved him away and protected her from his close scrutiny. The problem with it, however, was that her comment blocked his love from getting inside her where it could help heal her painful feelings of being unlovable. In fact she'd taken his love and slingshot it halfway across Ohio.

As it turned out, by the end of the day Linda got better at taking in Dave's fondness and admiration and gave him much of her own. And after swallowing some pride, I decided to leave that blasted bad therapeutic moment on film rather than editing it out. Might as well make this training film real rather than air-brushed.

My mistake had been not handling my own flooding well. Which makes the importance of our fifth principle eminently clear: Soothe yourself, then intervene. But how?, you might ask.

Let's begin with our own internal state. Most of us dislike being around boiling toxic energy. Quick! We want to grab the pot off the stove before all that hot mush boils over. Before we know it our hearts are off to the races, our armpits grow wet, our lungs barely whisper a breath, and we are flooded just like our clients.

We tell ourselves we have to calm down. We remind ourselves that we are the professionals; this isn't our fight, it's theirs; we don't have to be their saviors. But if these thoughts don't do it, what then? How do we really calm down so we can be our best therapeutic selves?

It's like that old saw we hear from airplane stewardesses: "Put on your own oxygen mask first before helping others with theirs."

John happens to have wonderful Vagal tone. Very little disrupts his equanimity. He is terrific at listening to couples' heated arguments. Mine can be tipped over by a feather. So it's been imperative to learn how to boost the ability of my Vagus to keep the brakes on so I don't get flooded and ruin the therapeutic moment.

After Linda came Lynette. Over months of work, she gave me many opportunities to try out ways to self-soothe. Sometimes they worked; sometimes they flopped. Of the many I tried, I culled the best ones and grabbed onto these when Lynette was at her fiery best. Thank goodness they grounded me so I could do decent work. Some of these techniques are as common as stoplights, and others are more personal. Here are my favorites:

1. First, pay attention to your own body and what parts tense up when you're in the midst of hostility. During later moments of hostility, direct your focus to those parts and relax them. For me, it's shoulders and jaws. My shoulders rise in fear, and my jaws clench with tension. So I'll purposely drop my shoulders and open my mouth slightly to loosen my jaw. This may have to be done repeatedly during a session, as tension can creep back in when I'm not looking.
2. Focus on your own breathing. Slow it down and deepen it. Counting to yourself might help. Inhale; exhale. Four counts in, four counts out. Make sure that as you inhale, your belly pushes out like a balloon filling up with air. As you exhale your belly should drop back down.
3. Pretend you're in a lab behind a one-way glass, just watching. It's a bit like trying to be John during those early years of discovery. Recall that he watched thousands of couples, not intervening but simply observing what they would do. To help yourself stay calm, try to take on an air of detachment and interest, just watching to see what this couple will do next. Will they calm themselves down? Will one of them shut down and stonewall? Will the other partner attempt to make a repair? And if he does, will she accept the repair and return to the discussion? Thoughts like these can stop

us from jumping in too fast, especially if we're flooded and want everything to be calmer RIGHT NOW.

4. Remember that the best intervention is often the smallest, one that is close to what they can already do, which makes it more reachable. Then learning it can almost feel like remembering. Think, "I don't have to be brilliant; I only have to help expand their skills a little bit at a time."
5. Identify a favorite tune that is soothing for you. Play it inside your head. "Row, Row, Row Your Boat," is one of mine. "Thirty bottles of beer on the wall," is one of John's.
6. Hold your own hand. Quietly stroke one hand with the thumb of the other hand.
7. See in your mind's eye an image of someone you love. I like to think of John, my beloved daughter, or sometimes my dog.
8. Imagine eating your favorite food. I like to envision digging into a hot fudge sundae with chocolate ice cream.
9. Bring up the image of a favorite place you've visited before and found beautiful and soothing. It could be a beach, a forest, a mountain pass, a sanctuary—any place will do. For a moment take yourself there and savor the memory.
10. When all else fails, here's one I'm slightly embarrassed to share but will anyway. When nothing else works I'll redesign one of my client's hairstyles or their wardrobe. Wouldn't she look great with a much shorter cut? Turquoise would look gorgeous on her with those skin tones. I bet he would look great with a mustache. Only do this for a moment or two, just to distract you from the decibels.

These are only a few suggestions. With a little experimentation, we're sure you'll find methods that can work even better for you.

Now let's return to our session.

Within seconds of ushering James and Lynette into my office, Lynette's voice takes on that abrasive edge. I know it's going to be another wild ride down the mountainside—the lava flow again. Again I have to avoid flooding if I'm going to help this couple. Calm down! (No, not that way—no exclamation marks.) Breathe and count, breathe and count. One bar of "Row, Row, Row Your Boat." Where's my other hand? Hold hands with myself. Don't clench them, silly. It'll be all right.

Then the eruption. Lynette leaps up, menacingly steps towards James, and cries out, "I can't get over this! You're still seeing her!" She sure looks tall and towering for someone so short.

I stand up, too, and face her a foot away from her angry eyes.

"Lynette, look at me. Just look at me, not at him. Focus on my eyes for a minute. Will you breathe with me? Just take a nice deep breath. That's right. Again. That's it. One more. Good. And another. That's it. Are you ready to sit down? Yes? Me, too. Now, tell me, what's going on?"

She does. It turns out James has lied to her again, saying he hasn't seen Sheryl (a past affair partner) when actually he has. The week before he had spotted her while bicycling on one of his favorite workout routes and incidentally, one of the places he used to rendezvous with his affair partners. He had stopped to chat. It lasted over an hour. A friend had seen them together and later called Lynette. No wonder she's furious.

I turn to James, "What kept you from telling Lynette about this?"

"I was scared."

"Of?"

"Of her going ballistic like she just did. I can't take it."

"Understandable. It's hard to hear words that sound like an attack. And yet when you don't tell the truth and hold onto secrets, she still can't trust you, right? If she finds out from somebody else, it's probably much worse. Like a double betrayal, where the first one is seeing and talking to an old affair partner, and the second one is choosing to lie and withhold that information from her."

"Yeah, I know. It was stupid."

"James, you're not stupid. But maybe that choice was less than your best."

After she's calm, Lynette joins in. With some guidance from me, she asks James, "Was this a planned meeting?"

"No, just a coincidence."

"How long did it last?"

"Maybe 45 minutes."

"What did you feel during it?"

"Sad."

"Why?"

"Well, to be honest, I know you're not going to want to hear this, but I guess I still have some feelings for her. It's not that I want to go back to her. Because I don't. I want us to work this out. Lynette, I'm really sorry. I just should have come to you and told you about it. I guess I'm a coward. But I don't want her. Please believe me. I love you."

Lynette stares hard at him.

I add, "Lynette, when there's been a longer affair, it's very common for the spouse to feel some sadness in breaking up with the affair partner. But I don't think James regrets the choice he's made to be with you just because he's grieving. He has repeatedly said he wants this marriage, and he wants you. That's what he's trying to tell you."

With a deep sigh she exhales, then relaxes a bit. The lava has cooled.

It's easy to imagine how things might have gone if I hadn't calmed myself down. In a worst-case scenario I might have stridently confronted James, even spit out, "What's the matter with you? Haven't you learned anything from me?" I can just see him furiously striding out my door and leaving Lynette and me in the dust, never to return.

As it was, James expressed remorse and more that day, acknowledging that he was still drawn to Sheryl but knowing he wanted his marriage more. By the session's end, he voiced his decision to write Sheryl a final good-bye with Lynette beside him as he did so. The next week, he proved true to his word.

Although the work with this couple was quite difficult, it was rendered easier by taking steps to calm myself down before intervening. Deep breathing combined with "Row, Row, Row Your Boat" is now one of my staples.

Any of the self-soothing methods mentioned here may or may not work for you. Better yet, they may spark your own creativity as you develop ones that personally work best for you. As you discover which ones serve you well, keep in mind that they should take only a number of seconds, maybe a minute at most. Ideally they shouldn't distract you from listening to your clients, tracking their dynamics, trying to hear their underlying themes and feelings, or thinking how best to intervene. These techniques should simply pave the way for you to remain your best therapeutic self: alert, focused, calm, empathetic, sensitive, and deeply caring for your clients rather than a flooded, overwhelmed, why-didn't-I-become-an-architect, why-do-I-do-this-to-myself, somebody-take-me-to-Pluto mess. We may have days when the latter is unavoidable. But hopefully, may they be far and few between.

Bringing It Into Practice

- Respect the power DPA has to rule a person's responses.
- Monitor your own physiological response and self-soothe if necessary.
- Experiment with your own methods for self-soothing and find one that works best for you.

6

THE SIXTH PRINCIPLE

Process Past Regrettable Incidents

Psychotherapy for couples is deeply rewarding, but it also confronts us with challenges. We need to help not one person but two, plus what lies between them. Partners we see often sit side by side like enemy ships, war-torn but still afloat. Many have fired rounds at each other, and there's been damage done. Some have blown open holes in each other's sides and maybe even sheared off a mast or two. In short, most have communicated badly for years and it shows.

In the strongest of relationships, that between mother and infant, Edward Tronick found that miscommunication occurs 70% of the time. That's like a .300 batting average, which is great in baseball. But in parenting relationships, it's hardly grounds for celebration. In adult romantic relationships, we do no better, and there's lots of room for regrettable incidents: missed signals, misunderstandings, and missed connections. We hear all about them in our sessions.

Couples tell us tales of how their partners have wronged them. When they offer a story, each hopes we'll swing onboard their ship and help them fire more rounds at their partner. The trouble is, we're not there to take sides. Instead, our job is to help them process negative incidents together so they can put them to rest. By *process* we mean to review a past event and talk calmly about how and why it went badly. If an incident is processed well, each partner comes to understand the other's perspective, feelings, and wounds, then takes responsibility for his or her mistakes and apologizes for them.

In our research we noticed that couples who process past regrettable incidents have relationships like iron compared with those who sweep them under the rug. Avoiders believe it's best to forgive, forget, and move on. But few couples can shake free of their bad memories. Painful images linger. The worst fester under the surface like an abscess that eventually infects the whole relationship.

Why can't couples let go of bad past interactions? We've looked to the great work of a little known Austrian psychologist to give us an answer.

Nearly a century ago, Bluma Zeigarnik lived and worked in Vienna. She had many questions about human memory and how it worked. One day while tucked away in a café sipping tea, she watched quietly as a bustling waiter served his customers. Without writing down a word, the waiter took complicated orders from 12 people at once, then scurried to the kitchen and delivered the orders to the chef. When he returned 20 minutes later with the orders piled high in his arms, he hadn't missed a single detail. Was he exceptional? No, all waiters in the café performed this well.

Zeigarnik did an experiment. Each time the waiters took an order, she tested their memory twice: before they delivered the order to the chef, and again immediately afterwards. Before passing orders on to the chef, the waiters recollected the orders perfectly. After the orders were delivered, they promptly forgot them. It seemed that once orders were fully processed, it was safe for the waiters to "wipe the board clean."

Inadvertently Zeigarnik had stumbled upon a fundamental law about memory, one that other studies have since confirmed: We humans can't let loose a memory until we've digested it, extracting all the meaning we can from it. Perhaps it is this tendency to chew on our experience like a dog on a bone, gleaning every last morsel of learning from it, that has helped us survive for so many centuries. Couples are no different. If a couple hasn't fully processed a searing incident between them, they can't let it go. But once they discuss it and grasp the mistakes they've made, their meanings and teachings, the incident can finally be laid to rest. Their processing extracts key lessons that are important to learn, and in turn these nourish the relationship's growth.

Many couples who come to therapy have regrettable incidents they have been shoving under the rug for years. The rug is so bumpy with rubble now that they can't walk three steps without tripping. They need our help to pull up the rug and clear out old hurts so they can have a smooth floor to stand on. It's best if we put a good tool in their hands so they can prevent debris from piling up in the first place. This is our sixth principle for doing effective couples therapy: process past regrettable incidents.

When partners fight badly or miscommunicate, usually they both end up hurt. Unfortunately, when they try to process it later, poor communication sticks to them like a stubborn stain. The biggest mistake partners make is to stay invested in proving they are right and their partner is wrong. Only this time they will fight over which partner has the best memory and recollects the past more accurately. But under the surface, they'll be really tangling over a different issue: which one is most entitled to feel hurt. The winner gets to wear the victim title, while the loser is labeled bad, selfish, or mean. Misguided, they assume there is only one truth, and each one claims to possess it. This assumption keeps them locked in battle, and it's wrong.

There are always two points of view about what happens in an interaction, and both viewpoints make some sense. If we ask two people sitting across from each other to draw a girl who sits between them, they'll come up with two different sketches. And both will be accurate. They're simply seeing her from two different angles and drawing what they see. Likewise, when couples argue or miscommunicate, they're living an experience through two sets of eyes, ears, and minds that interpret input differently. Regardless of what words they hear, everything gets filtered through each person's history and experience. Consequently no two people will hear a sentence the same way. The words may be identical, but not their meanings. And the more the words are laden with emotion, the more room there is for distortion. Thus one cheerful partner will say the sky is a lovely blue, while the other one, full of fears, will see it black as night and threatening thunder.

Processing a past regrettable incident is complicated. We've learned what works well by observing how the masters of relationship do it. Typically they process a past incident as if they're audience members sitting up high in a theater balcony during intermission, calmly discussing what happened during the first act. They start with two underlying assumptions. First, they assume that their viewpoints will differ about what happened, and *both will be right*. Second, they know that an apology will be meaningless unless the partner stating it understands fully what he or she is apologizing for.

To begin with, each partner takes a turn to express his or her point of view about what happened while the other partner listens. When speaking, each one digs deep to unearth feelings, states of mind, and old wounds that may have been torn open again. The listener works hard to empathize. Only after each partner has fully understood the other's experience do they finally voice their remorse and apologize.

John and I understand how crucial it is to process past regrettable incidents, since we've been married for nearly 30 years with too many of them to count! We've had lots of opportunities to practice. About five years ago, we designed a five-step intervention to help our distressed clients and ourselves, too. It's taken some tweaking to get it just right. Now in small booklet format, we use it in all our couples' workshops and our clinical sessions as needed. Here is the text from it:

AFTERMATH OF A FIGHT OR REGRETTABLE INCIDENT

Five steps to reclaiming goodwill with your partner

This form is for "processing" past fights, regrettable incidents, or past emotional injuries.

"Processing" means that you can talk about the incident without getting back into it again. It needs to be a conversation—as if you were both sitting in the balcony of a theater looking down on the stage where the action had occurred. This requires calm and some emotional distance from the incident.

Before you begin

Keep in mind the goal is greater understanding–addressing the process and *how* the issue was talked about, without getting back into the fight. So wait until you're both calm.

We assume that *each* of your realities has validity. Perception is everything. Don't focus on "the facts."

Pay attention to the common barriers to communication and their antidotes as you move through the process. The Four Horsemen reference can help.

Work through the following five steps together.

THE FIVE STEPS

1. *Feelings:* Share how you felt. Do not say why you felt that way. Avoid commenting on your partner's feelings.
2. *Realities:* Describe your reality. Take turns. Summarize and validate at least a part of your partner's reality.
3. *Triggers:* Share what experiences or memories you've had that might have escalated the interaction, and the stories of why these are triggers for each of you.
4. *Responsibility:* Acknowledge your own role in contributing to the fight or regrettable incident.
5. *Constructive Plans:* Plan together one way that each of you can make it better next time.

Step 1: Feelings

Share how you felt, but not why yet.

(Read aloud the items that were true for you during the fight. Do not comment on your partner's feelings.)

I felt:

1. defensive
2. not listened to
3. feelings got hurt
4. totally flooded
5. angry
6. sad
7. unloved
8. misunderstood
9. criticized
10. took a complaint personally
11. like you didn't even like me
12. not cared about
13. worried
14. afraid
15. unsafe
16. tense
17. I was right and you were wrong
18. both of us were partly right
19. out of control
20. frustrated
21. righteously indignant
22. morally justified
23. unfairly picked on
24. unappreciated
25. disliked
26. unattractive
27. stupid
28. morally outraged

29. taken for granted
30. like leaving
31. like staying and talking this through
32. I was overwhelmed with emotion
33. not calm
34. stubborn
35. powerless
36. I had no influence
37. I wanted to win this one
38. my opinions didn't even matter
39. there was a lot of give and take
40. I had no feelings at all
41. I had no idea what I was feeling
42. lonely
43. alienated
44. ashamed
45. guilty
46. culpable
47. abandoned
48. disloyal
49. exhausted
50. foolish
51. overwhelmed
52. remorseful
53. shocked
54. tired

Step 2: Realities

Subjective Reality and Validation

1. Take turns describing your perceptions, your own reality of what happened during the regrettable incident. Describe yourself and your perception. Don't describe your partner. Avoid attack and blame. Talk about what you might have needed from your part-

ner. Describe your perceptions like a reporter, giving an objective blow-by-blow description. Say "I heard you saying," rather than "You said."

2. Summarize and then validate your partner's reality by saying something like, "It makes sense to me how you saw this and what your perceptions and needs were. I get it." Use empathy by saying something like, "I can see why this upset you." Validation doesn't mean you agree, but that you can understand even a part of your partner's experience of the incident.
3. Do both partners feel understood? If yes, move on. If no, ask, "What do I need to know to understand your perspective better?" After summarizing and validating, ask your partner, "Did I get it?" and "Is there anything else?"

Step 3: Triggers

- Share what escalated the interaction for you. What events in the interaction triggered a big reaction in you?
- As you rewind the video tape of your memory, stop at a point where you had a similar set of feelings triggered in the past. Now tell the story of that past moment to your partner, so your partner can understand why that is a trigger for you.
- Share your stories. It will help your partner understand you. As you think about your early history or childhood, is there a story you remember that relates to what got triggered in you, your "enduring vulnerabilities"? Your partner needs to know you, so that your partner can be more sensitive to you.

Examples of triggers:

1. I felt judged. I'm very sensitive to that.
2. I felt excluded. I'm very sensitive to that.
3. I felt criticized. I'm very sensitive to that.
4. I felt flooded.
5. I felt ashamed.

6. I felt lonely.
7. I felt belittled
8. I felt disrespected.
9. I felt powerless.
10. I felt out of control.
11. Other:

Validation

Does any part of your partner's triggers and story make sense to you?

Step 4: Take Responsibility

Under ideal conditions, you might have done better at talking about this issue.

1. *What set me up for the miscommunication*

Share how you set yourself up to get into this conflict. Read aloud the items that were true for you on this list:

What set me up:

1. I've been very stressed and irritable lately.
2. I've not expressed much appreciation towards you lately.
3. I've taken you for granted.
4. I've been overly sensitive lately.
5. I've been overly critical lately.
6. I've not shared very much of my inner world.
7. I've not been emotionally available.
8. I've been turning away more.
9. I've been getting easily upset.
10. I've been depressed lately.
11. I've had a chip on my shoulder lately.
12. I've not been very affectionate.
13. I've not made time for good things between us.
14. I've not been a very good listener lately.
15. I've not asked for what I needed.

16. I've been feeling a bit like a martyr.
17. I've needed to be alone.
18. I've not wanted to take care of anybody.
19. I have been very preoccupied.
20. I haven't felt very much confidence in myself.
21. I've been running on empty.

2. Specifically what do you regret, and specifically what was your contribution to this regrettable incident or fight?

3. What do you wish to apologize for?

(Read aloud)
I'm sorry that:

- I overreacted.
- I was really grumpy.
- I was defensive.
- I was so negative.
- I attacked you.
- I didn't listen to you.
- I wasn't respectful.
- I was unreasonable.
- Other:

4. If you accept your partner's apology, say so. If not, say what you still need.

Step 5: Constructive Plans

Share one thing *your partner* can do to make a discussion of this issue better next time. (It's important to remain calm as you do this.)

Then, while it's still your turn, share one thing *you* can do to make it better next time.

What do you need to be able to put this behind you and move on? Be as agreeable as possible to the plans suggested by your partner.

Here's how this exercise works: When a couple reports they've had a regrettable incident, we ask if they would like to learn how to process the incident so they can put it behind them. If the answer is "yes," we hand them the booklet. First, we explain the assumption that in every incident there are always two points of view; both right. Then we guide them step by step through the process.

Despite having a structure to follow, this intervention can still be challenging. Sometimes it's tough for *us* to adhere to the "two-points-of-view" assumption. We may resonate with one partner's version of a story more than the other's. Or perhaps our lifetime experience may mirror that partner's history. We may be more attracted to one partner's personality. One partner's story may tug harder on our sympathies. All of these may compel us to take a side. But for both partners to feel safe enough to expose their vulnerabilities to each other, they have to feel safe with us. Our empathy is their safety net. When they each explain their points of view, if their partner doesn't catch their drift, they hope at least we will. So we have to stretch ourselves like a bungee cord to empathize fairly. And the greater their pain, the more we must expand ourselves so we can embrace them both.

In our opinion, no one is better at empathizing with couples than Dan Wile. He's a clinical psychologist practicing in Oakland, California, the author of several books for clinicians, and lucky for us, a good friend. In order to dissolve attack-defend patterns in partners, Wile speaks for his clients as if he's their voice. After one speaks, he swings his chair beside him or her, looks into the other partner's eyes, and speaks the words he imagines the first one feels. First he replaces any venom from the partner's original phrasing with kinder and more transparent wording. He may also include words of love, admiration, and respect that were muted earlier, or the fear, grief, and pain cowering behind the partner's facade. The message that emerges is washed clean of hostility but stays true to the original message. After finishing he always checks in with the partner to make sure he's gotten it right. If not, he humbly alters his wording to better match the partner's intent. Once his compassionate restatement has warmed the air, he steps back and encourages the couple to resume their dialogue.

Wile has told us he always chooses the partner he has the toughest time empathizing with to be the one he speaks for first. Later will come the one he can relate to more easily. He's like a swimmer who dives into a murky river first before gliding into clear waters ahead.

Let's look at a case where Wile's method proved invaluable. Derek and Stephan needed to work on processing a regrettable incident. Here is their story:

Derek loved to have sex and wanted it daily with Stephan. He thought sex cemented their emotional connection. But Stephan disagreed. Without emotionally connecting before lovemaking, he thought sex equaled pornography—exciting but empty. For Stephan emotional connection came first, but for Derek, sex should come first, with emotions later (or never): a classic chicken and egg dilemma that left them both broken, fried, and unsatisfied.

Derek epitomized toughness. With huge biceps, a neck wider than his head and thighs like jackhammers, he was the kind of guy you would hate to meet in a dark alley. But beneath the muscles, he was quite fragile. He'd grown up a military brat with a dad who was an iron-fisted army lifer. The family had moved every two years. Whenever he started at a new school, Derek always had to prove himself by nailing the class bully against some shadowy back wall. Afterwards he'd be left alone to roam the hills in peace. He rarely made friends.

At home it was another story. Now and then, Dad's PTSD would tornado into their kitchen, leaving Dad cowering under the table in fear or swinging fists at whoever was near. His symptoms would mount like a tidal wave hitting shore and he'd drown in them. His work would soon deteriorate and before long, the family would be transferred to another base.

During these episodes, Derek learned to drift out the back door and wander until the danger had passed. Meanwhile his mom withstood the storms like a lone pine, silent and strong. She couldn't nurture Derek, but she was constant.

Around age 12, as Derek's hormones pumped voltage into his veins, he noticed boys, not girls. When he fell for his math teacher, he was transfixed by the danger of his difference. His isolation thickened with time.

After high school he moved to Seattle and worked in construction. There he found men like himself who loved other men. Finally he could raise his eyes from the sidewalk. One night at a party, he lifted his gaze and found Stephan.

Stephan's story was different. Raised in the American heartland by a single mom, he was bullied and taunted from age six on. Slight and slender, he possessed the sensitivity of an angel. At school he was surrounded by calloused farm boys who tossed around bales of hay like bundles of feathers. He didn't stand a chance. The boys would encircle him like hyenas, laughing, then darting in for the kill. Again and again he'd come home with blood on his shirt and rips in his jeans.

Mom pleaded with school officials to intervene, to no avail. They scoffed at her worries, gave her the infuriating, "Boys will be boys," and sent her on her way. Chained to her waitressing job for money, she tried to comfort Stephan but couldn't protect him. He learned to fold up like a fan. There was less body surface to hit that way. So he endured.

Stephan was smart, especially in math. After high school, he attended a college that was a harbor for brainy outcasts. There he joined a men's a capella group. For the first time, he felt warmed by people other than his mother.

Upon graduation, Stephan got a job with an Internet company in Seattle. In the progressive exuberance of the city, he found new friends, new lovers, and then a few years later, the love of his life, Derek. At last he'd found his knight.

Derek and Stephan moved in together a few months after meeting. They settled into a daily rhythm, always parting every morning and reuniting later with kisses. Over dinners, Stephan loved their conversation. Chatting away, he would share the baubles and burdens of his day. But after a year together, Derek seemed to be bored and responded with only a word or two. Stephan grew frustrated. He tried to draw out Derek with questions about workmates, clients, gym gossip, anything and everything. Nothing worked. Derek didn't want to talk. He'd voice a few monosyllables and then later, push Stephan to have sex. At first, Stephan was happy to do so. But this pattern grew old. Then, beyond old. Stephan began to dread the after-dinner dance. Derek seemed inexhaustible. As their silence deepened, Stephan's mood darkened, too. He stopped asking questions. He dawdled over the dishes. He drifted into computer games, dwelling on them long after Derek retired to bed. He pulled the shade down over his heart. Their lovemaking dropped to once a week, once a month, then nothing.

After three months of nothing, the fighting began in earnest. During one terrible incident when Stephan had once again refused sex, Derek hurled insults at him. "You lost your balls at work today? You're like dirt. Why don't you just dry up and blow away?"

Stephan slung back a few of his own. "No brain left after work today? All you know how to do is screw. You've got no soul. You wouldn't know real love if it smacked you," to which Derek furiously slammed the door, shaking loose its hinges as he stormed out for the night.

Three weeks later, they sat in my office, staring holes in the walls. We began with assessment. Clearly their conflict management was a mess. Terrible fights had ruined their romance and friendship. They conflicted by either battling verbally or pretending their partner didn't exist. Yet there was still that palpable yearning for connection, like two planets pulled close by some ineffable gravity.

One day they shared the story of a fight they'd had earlier in the week. Derek had come home late. On his way home he had thought about trying to initiate sex even though he felt pretty hopeless about it. He had found Stephan on his computer. He had greeted him, but Stephan ignored him, not even saying hello. He had tried again. Still no response. Finally his frustration and rage had broken through and they'd had a terrible row.

I empathized with how painful the fight must have been for both of them and then explained that when a couple experiences a troubling incident but chooses to avoid discussing it, the memory of the event becomes like a stone in your shoe, impossible to ignore or forget and hurting with every step. The event will linger like a bone-deep bruise, refusing to heal. William Faulkner captured it well when he wrote, "The past is never dead. In fact, it isn't even past."

"Would you like to try talking about this one?" I asked tentatively. "It might help you understand what happened so it can stop hurting this much."

"I guess," Stephan mumbled.

"Whatever," Derek muttered.

To help them structure their discussion, they each got a copy of our booklet, "The Aftermath of a Fight or Regrettable Incident.". I explained the content and suggested they begin with Step 1. Taking turns, each one would read over a list of emotions and say out loud which ones they'd felt during the fight. They didn't have to limit how many they named. I cautioned them to not say why they had the feelings now. That would come later. Stephan went first.

"Angry, hurt, defensive, afraid, unsafe, tense, frustrated, overwhelmed with emotion, I was right and you were wrong, unloved, sad, unattractive, like you didn't even like me, ashamed, frightened, alone."

Derek sighed. It was his turn. "Umm, angry, defensive . . . like you didn't even like me, tense, flooded, hurt, stupid, unattractive, alienated I guess . . . Very alone. . . ."

A pause.

Onto Step 2: "Each of you will take a turn being the speaker while your partner is the listener. When you're the speaker, tell your point of view about what happened, step by step, from the beginning to the end." I added the underlying assumption of two points of view being true in every incident.

"The tricky part here is to not criticize or blame your partner while you're speaking. Try to describe the facts of your experience like the facts in a newspaper story. Then tie the facts to what you felt and how you responded. Here's where you get to explain *why* you felt some particular emotion. Let me give you an example. It may sound like this: 'I heard you say you couldn't stand me. I felt really hurt by that. Then I wanted to hurt you back. So I said, "You make me sick." Then I saw this angry look on your face and I felt afraid.' And so on. So, the facts, plus your feelings and response. After the speaker is finished, it's the listener's job to briefly summarize what you've heard the speaker say and then—the hard part—try to put yourself in your partner's shoes and say something that validates your partner's point of view. . . something like, 'okay, I get it, I can understand how you might feel that way,' or 'From your point of view that makes sense to me.' Words like these don't mean you agree with your partner's point of view. They just mean that from *his* perspective, you can understand how he experienced things like he did. Does this make sense?"

They both nodded.

"All right, who wants to start?"

"Me," Derek said.

He began. "I want to start with some background. We hadn't had sex in a long time. Whenever I asked for it, you said, 'Not now,' or 'I don't feel like it. Maybe tomorrow.' Only when tomorrow came, there was nothing. Pretty soon it was months without it. I didn't see the point of even coming home. I hung out at the gym longer. I thought maybe if I did, you'd miss me. I didn't really know what to do. I just got more and more frustrated. And maybe a little depressed. I didn't know what was wrong. I figured it must be me. Maybe you just didn't feel attracted to me anymore. Or care. Maybe you'd found somebody else at work, one of those brainiacs. I can't compete with those guys. I began to think, 'Why is he with me, anyway? I should just move on.' But deep down, I didn't want to. Anyway, I wasn't sleeping well. I worried a lot. Then you stopped talking to me. Then you stopped even looking at me. What was the point? I felt really hopeless. So pretty soon I would stop at this bar on the way home, have a shot or two. That night we're talking about, I think I had three. I got home pretty late. You were sitting at your stupid computer, playing one of those stupid games."

I interrupted, "Derek, can you tone down the criticism, please?"

"Yeah, okay. So you were at your computer. I couldn't see what you were doing. Actually I guess I was afraid you were in some chat room, or maybe Skyping with some other dude. I started to get angry. I remember saying something like, 'What the hell are you doing?' And I think you said, 'What do you think I'm doing?' And I said, 'Oh I suppose f—-ing around with some asshole online like you always do.' I was really pissed. You glared at me and said, 'How dare you? You have no right to say that.' I said, 'I've got every right in the book, you ball-less hypocrite. If I'm not getting it, somebody must be. So who is it? That skinny twerp with the thick glasses? He's probably all you can get.' You said, 'What's that supposed to mean?' I didn't really know. I was just mad. I think I said some more things, but I don't remember them now. After that, I headed out the door and slammed it hard to show you how mad I was. I went back to the bar and sat there until it closed. Then I just wandered the streets. I didn't want to come home."

Derek's shoulders slumped. No tears, just dead silence. His sadness filled the room. He looked defeated, like a dazed soldier stumbling past a fallen body. There was so much pain here. I wanted to give him more of a voice.

"Would you consider letting me speak for you, Derek? I'd like to expand a little on what you've just said. Would that be all right?"

"Yeah, sure."

My chair is one of those big wingback, hulking things that doesn't move easily. So I kneel beside partners I'm speaking for. This pays them respect, shows I give them authority, and can offer a feeling of alliance.

Kneeling beside Derek, images arose of his early barren life, the isolation and self-doubts, and the years spent drifting from school to school, relying only on his physical strength for a living.

"Stephan, I've really missed you. When we eat together, I listen. I try to follow along. But sometimes you talk so fast that I have trouble keeping up. I get anxious. Your words become a blur, and I don't know what to say. You sound so smart, witty, funny. I'm afraid that if I open my mouth and say anything I'll say something really stupid. And then you'll see that I've got half your intelligence, no education to speak of, and nothing important to contribute. And then you'll despise me. I'm so afraid I'm not good enough for you. I don't read like you do, I barely know how to do email let alone the fancy stuff you do on the computer, and it seems crazy that I could actually be with someone as smart as you. I really worry about it sometimes. And I see you looking at me, wanting to hear something great from me, and then it really gets bad. I get a big knot in my stomach and my mouth goes dry and I can't even say my own name. But I'm dying to touch you. I look at you and you are so beautiful to me. You're so gentle. Sometimes when I hold you I'm afraid you'll break. All I have to give you is my body.

"I feel so helpless. Every time you reject me I feel like I have nothing to give. It's like those times in the kitchen with Dad when he'd be under the table again, surrounded by his demons. I'd feel so terrible. I'd want to take his hand, usher him out of his own hell, and bring him to me. But it was impossible. If I got too close I'd get hit. So I learned to keep my distance, keep safe, watch him drown, and just hope beyond hope that he'd see me for what I was, a scared kid dying to connect with him, to be held by him, to just reach him somehow. But there was no way. I was completely helpless to span that space between us. He felt as far away as a ship at sea. That's how you felt to me that night. So far away, just staring at your computer. I had no idea of how to reach you, tell you I need you, tell you that you mean everything to me. I didn't know what words to use to draw you near. And then I just got mad. Mad that you didn't hear me calling you. I know that seems crazy because mostly I was just being silent. But honestly, what could I say to you that would draw your attention to me and make you want to be with me? I didn't know. So I reached for you in the only way I could, with my body. At least I thought my body was okay, pretty decent. You used to like it. I just wanted our bodies to touch, to feel that rush of passion that I love so much and to just lose myself in our sex together. But there was no bridge to you, at least none that I knew how to cross. So when you didn't respond or look up, I felt invisible, worthless. Probably the drinks I had made it worse. Then something just snapped. When I yelled insults at you, I knew it was wrong. I guess I was trying to get you to feel how I felt at that moment, the one without balls, the one who has nothing to offer. The worst part about it was at that moment I was just like my dad, striking out blindly and just wanting to hurt you. Then I felt deeply ashamed of what I was becoming. So then I took myself out the door, back into that isolation that was always my escape as a kid. It didn't help much, but at least it was old and familiar. Alone again. . . . Was that about right, Derek?"

He nodded. I went back to my chair.

"Stephan, can you try to summarize what's been said?"

Stephan replied, "Well . . . so you haven't known how to respond to me when I talk to you at night. You haven't felt that, I guess, you were smart enough to have anything to say that I would want to hear. Sometimes you just feel stupid. That's terrible, Derek. I really didn't know that. I was just trying to reach out to you by talking to you."

"Just try to stay with Derek's reality now, Stephan," I whisper. "You'll get to tell him yours as soon as it's your turn to be the speaker."

"So that night, you came home late and found me on my computer. You felt insecure, like I was connecting with somebody else, some other guy maybe. That made you mad, but really you were hurting. Inside you wanted to have sex. But it was very clear to you that I didn't. Then you felt even more rejected. You felt invisible like you did at home sometimes. Like your dad couldn't see you and what you were going through when he was under that table. So you said some harsh things and then I got upset and said some harsh things back. That hurt you more. But it also sounds like you felt helpless. You didn't know how to reach me. Maybe you felt hopeless. Then you left the apartment because it was clear that nothing good was going to happen between us. For sure, no sex. But also nothing, no connection. Have I got it right?"

"Yeah, that's it."

"Stephan," I asked, "Is there any part of Derek's reality that makes sense to you? Could you say some words that are validating for him, for what he went through?"

"For sure. I get that you felt invisible, that you felt really terrible because we hadn't been connecting and I rejected you in the way you could connect best with me. I really understand that. It makes sense to me."

"Good, Stephan."

I turned to Derek, "Are you ready to hear Stephan's reality now?" Derek nodded.

"It's pretty simple, actually," Stephan said. "I'd tried for months to just talk with you, to just tell you about my day, to just have a decent conversation. But the more I tried, the more distant we got. I began to feel that aloneness, too. That night you came home really late, like ten o'clock or something. That was really different for you. You weren't usually at the gym that late. So I actually thought you might have been hooking up with somebody from there, some hunk who could give you what you wanted. That wouldn't be so bad, except that I really missed you. But without you I went on my computer like I usually do when you're not home and was just Facebooking with some friends. On Facebook I tell friends what's happening, tell somebody I'm alive. It seemed like you didn't care at all about me. I just wanted to be asked, 'How was your day? What happened for you today?' But I never heard that. I felt hopeless, too. So getting back to when you came home, I looked up and you looked angry. You were frowning like I'd done something wrong. So immediately my shields went up. I thought, 'Oh boy, here comes another fight.' I didn't want to fight. I was tired. So your words hit me like a punch in the face. It felt so unfair. All I was doing was sitting at my computer and out of nowhere comes this blow. It scared me. I didn't know what you were going to do. Plus I could smell that you'd been drinking. That scared me even more. I just wanted to get away from you, to protect myself. But there was nowhere to go. I hoped the things I said would make you leave. And they did. But after you left, I felt terrible. Like I was a hopeless failure, like I wasn't worth anything. I got pretty agitated. I remember getting up and walking around and around, carving a path in the carpet. It felt so bad. That's it, I guess."

It was time to switch roles and try speaking for Stephan.

Resting next to him I said, "When we first got together I loved your coming home to me. I loved making you those great meals, watching you scarf them up, knowing you loved them and loved me. I loved lying next to you, feeling your strength and your power and your body. But after a while things became more routine. I wanted us to be like one of those older couples who sits over dinner and laughs, telling each other stories from their days, finishing each other's sentences, just loving being together inhaling the same air. I wanted that easy comfort with you. I know I'd chatter on like some magpie, but that was my way of bringing you into my world. I didn't care that you might not understand all the tech stuff. That's irrelevant to me. I just wanted you to show you were interested, to ask me questions, to compare what happened with me to where you'd been all day. I wanted to hear your stories about the idiots you were building for, the ways they'd change all the blueprints at the last minute so you'd want to tear your hair out. I wanted to hear what your buddies were telling you as you had lunch together. I wanted to even hear how it was at the gym, though I'd never set foot in that place, just because that was your world and I wanted to know it better, know you better—like everyday sit behind your eyes, seeing what you saw and hearing what you heard. But that never happened. I'd try to invite you into my world, but it never worked. It didn't seem like you were interested or even curious about it. So I got worried. I hoped something would change. But I couldn't make love to you. How could I? I didn't even know who you were anymore. I just wanted closeness. That's what makes me feel sexual. I didn't just want to be your porn star. I wanted to be your lover, the man you *knew* and *then* loved. I wanted your comfort, your concern, your admiration, your appreciation. Just connection! Something beyond just our bodies.

"That night when you came home you scared me to death. You looked furious. I was just making contact with friends, nothing sexual, but then I heard you accusing me of disloyalty. I began to shake inside. I didn't know what you'd do. Then out came the insults. But they were worse than that. I felt kicked in the gut. It was just like high school all over again with those jocks pounding on me. Jumping on me from out of nowhere and there was nothing I could do about it, nowhere to run, no escape. I was terrified. High school, it all came back. I looked at your eyes and you looked like you wanted to kill me. And the alcohol I smelled. That made it terrifying. When those high school jocks were drunk it was always so much worse. The hitting wouldn't stop. I'd think I was going to die . . . anyway, I really thought you might hit me. I said some mean stuff back. I wanted to run out, but you were between me and the door. So when you left, I was relieved. It had felt so close to violence. But after the door slammed, the despair hit. I felt myself sinking down into this bleak, black place. I was so alone nothing could pull me out of it. It was awful. I had no idea of what to do. So I just curled up and waited. Helpless, hopeless."

Stephan turned his face into the couch.

"Okay?" I asked.

"Okay."

Derek spoke. "I see it now. You wanted to talk with me. I guess it didn't matter whether I said stupid things or not. You just wanted me to listen and to be interested. And to tell stories, even though I'm not much of a talker. So when I didn't, you thought I didn't care. And when I didn't care, or so you thought, you didn't want to be sexual with me. Because then it would feel too cold, like you were just my toy or something. Too impersonal. And that night when you looked at me and saw how angry I was you got scared. You didn't know what I'd do. You thought I might do something violent, like those guys around you in high school. Geez. You were afraid of me. That's who I looked like to you—one of those guys. So you shot insults at me. Oh yeah, you also said my words felt unfair to you, because you were just on Facebook and not doing anything sexual with anybody else. So my words really hurt. When I left, you felt better. You were out of danger. I know that feeling really good."

"Did he get it right, Stephan?" I asked.

"Yup."

"And now some validation, Derek?"

"It's not too hard to figure out. You were scared. I understand that. And you felt slugged by the insults. I know. They felt unfair to me, too, but at the time I didn't care. Sorry, Steph."

"We'll get there, Derek," I replied.

We spent the remaining time completing the steps in the booklet. They explored more of what had gotten triggered for each of them. Finally both partners owned up to their mistakes and apologized for them. They finished up by planning how to prevent a similar incident from happening in the future. Derek would work on sharing more of himself; Stephan would make sure he greeted Derek at night. They would both practice describing feelings, not trading insults. At first separate and alone, Derek and Stephan had returned home to each other. The memory of this fight would soon fade away.

Derek and Stephan were an unusual match. Stephan, verbal, Derek, nonverbal. Stephan, technical, Derek, physical. Perhaps they loved in the other what they yearned for in themselves. But as time passed, Derek opened again to Stephan, learning it wasn't vocabulary his partner wanted but entry into his world; that was enough. And as Derek allowed Stephan closer, Stephan returned sexually to Derek. That was what Derek wanted most. They found comfort in each other.

After their processing session, I sat still in the quiet. Waves of their pain slapped against my insides. First one side, then the other. Gradually the waves merged, counterbalanced, calmed one another, then finally smoothed out and drifted together into one stream.

Bringing It Into Practice

- A structured dialogue can help couples to process past regrettable incidents
- There are always two points of view in every fight and both are right.
- Partners need to understand each other's feelings and perceptions about what happened.
- Partners should take responsibility for their specific contributions to regrettable incidents.
- Processing incidents can provide insight into each person's inner world.
- Partners should make a plan for how to prevent a similar incident from happening in the future.

7

THE SEVENTH PRINCIPLE

Replace the Four Horsemen with Gentle Conflict Management Skills

Let's talk about couples that have been arguing nonstop for months. The worst ones rage out of control like a forest fire. Now their battles threaten to burn their Relationship House to the ground.

Over the past four decades John has studied nearly a thousand couples like these. Their conflict discussions are riddled with problems. Perpetually at war, they will do almost anything to win. Sometime while fighting, they will call up the big guns, the Four Horsemen of the Apocalypse: criticism, contempt, defensiveness, and stonewalling. The first two they use as weapons, the last two as shields. Here's a typical example of how they may sound:

HUSBAND: Did you pay the bills today?

WIFE: How come it's my job all of a sudden?

HUSBAND: Because you're the one who spends all our money.

I just want you to see how deep you're getting us in debt. Actually, you're destroying our credit single-handedly. . . . You didn't pay them, right?

WIFE: Look, if you weren't such a loser at your lousy, low-paying job we'd have plenty of money to go around and no problem with the bills.

HUSBAND: Oh, so it's my fault now, huh? What about the $500 you spent on clothes last month? What do you think I am, made of money? Why don't *you* go out and get a job instead of sitting on your fat ass all day?

WIFE: Fine, you take care of our four kids and do all the cooking and cleaning and laundry and I'd be happy to get a job. *Loser*!

What's happening here? He starts off with a fairly innocuous question ("Did you pay the bills?"). But she smells criticism and responds defensively ("How come it's my job?"). And she's right; he is being critical. Next he throws a sharper knife at her ("You're destroying our credit"). She responds by shielding herself with more defensiveness but this time heaps some contempt on top of it ("If you weren't such a loser"). This leads him to ratchet up his defensiveness ("What about the $500 you spent on clothes?") and catapult contempt back at her ("sitting on your fat ass"). Obviously, they accomplish nothing but emotional injury. Enough bonfires like this and love burns down to ash.

Our job is to stop the conflagration. But how? Some therapists like to step in and problem solve for their couples. Couples may feel better afterwards, but they haven't learned how to problem solve for themselves without the therapist's help. Other therapists have each person summarize what their partner is saying in order to slow things down and improve listening. This can be useful. However, it won't be if the therapist doesn't also attend to how the speaker is voicing his complaints. We once saw a film of a therapist working with a couple in which the husband said to his wife, "You are such a slob. I hate all the messes you make. What's the matter with you?" The therapist instructed the wife to reply, "I see. You are angry with me. Tell me more." Really? Who wants to hear more about what a slob they are? The effect of the therapist's instructions is to collude with the husband's abuse. It's crucial that we address not only how partners respond to one another but also how they speak to each other in the first place. Criticism and contempt do not work. Only someone like the Dalai Lama, who meditates hours a day, can calmly respond to words like "slob" or "What's the matter with you?" And he's not married.

Couples want to sustain a strong Relationship House. To help them avoid burning the house down with out-of-control conflicts, we need to teach them how to manage their own conflicts. We need to be sure the methods we teach them are both realistic and doable without us.

This is our seventh principle for doing effective couples therapy: replace the Four Horsemen with gentle conflict management skills.

To know how to help our clients, let's talk in more detail about the Four Horsemen of the Apocalypse, those big predictors of relationship demise that John identified in his research. We'll add the skills needed to rein them in.

The first predictor is criticism, or blaming a relationship problem on a personality flaw of the partner's. This is where words like *lazy*, *dumb*, *selfish*, and *thoughtless* get used. Even phrases like "You never . . ." or "You always . . ." are criticisms, since a person who never does anything right or always does something wrong probably has something personally wrong with her. We've noticed that the masters of relationships try hard to censor words like these. But they aren't perfect. Occasionally they, too, blurt out a criticism. But then they repair the hurt of it by quickly apologizing to their partner and softening their next statement.

When relationship masters carefully raise a complaint, they start by stating their feelings. First they say, "I feel . . . [some emotion]." If they can't identify a specific emotion, they say something like "I'm upset," or "I'm stressed." Second, they describe the situation that has evoked the emotion without blaming their partner for it. In other words, they describe *what* has caused their feelings, not *who*. Third, they conclude by saying what they need to feel better. This gives their partner an opportunity to shine for them. When describing their request, they often add concrete details to make their needs as clear as possible. For example, instead of stating, "I need you to be more responsible," they say, "I need you to pay the bills tonight." And if they're super-masters, they frame their need as a polite question, like "Would you please pay the bills tonight?"

The second step, describing the situation, is often the sticky part of phrasing as the description can covertly imply that the partner who is listening has done something wrong and is still being subtly criticized. For example, if I say to John, "I'm upset that the dishes have been badly washed again," there's a subtle hint that John is a bad dishwasher. However, doing something badly at a given time is different than being bad all the time. If I wanted to be really critical, I could say something like, "I'm upset that you're too careless to get the dishes clean," or "You always do a terrible job washing the dishes." Words like *careless* or phrases like "you always" are more critical of John's character. If I want him to hear my complaint and respond nondefensively, the softer approach will work better than criticism.

We named the healthier method of voicing complaints "Gentle Start-Up,", as opposed to "Harsh Start-Up", where criticism and contempt rule the airwaves.

In analyzing conflict discussion start-ups, John and his colleagues made an amazing discovery: The first three minutes of a conflict conversation can be used to predict not only how the rest of the conversation will go but also how the rest of the relationship will go six years down the road . . . with high accuracy! In other words, the way a couple raises a complaint almost perfectly predicts whether their relationship will succeed or fail six years later. If we help couples soften the way they raise complaints by using gentle start-up rather than harsh start-up, we can give them a far better chance at future happiness.

Let's look at examples of Harsh Start-Up versus Gentle Start-Up.

George is worried about his mother-in-law coming over for dinner tonight because she always finds something about him to criticize. He wants his wife to support him if that happens again. Think how his wife will respond if he starts off with this: "Dear, your mother is a wart on the back of humanity." A Harsh Start-Up, this probably won't elicit an outpouring of her support.

Instead he could say: "Honey, I'm worried about your mom coming over tonight. She can get pretty critical of me. Would you please stand up for me if she does?"

"Worried" is the feeling; "About your mom coming over tonight . . . she can get critical with me," is the situation he's worried about, and, "Would you please stand up for me?" is what he needs.

Chances are, George's wife will have an easier time hearing his Gentle Start-Up than "mom" and "warts" in the same sentence. She might even feed him dinner rather than grabbing her mom's hand, huffing out the door, and leaving George to feed himself.

Here's another example: Carol is worried about having enough money to pay the bills. She wants Leslie to ask for a raise at work. She could use this Harsh Start-Up: "I just know you're too much of a wimp to ask for a raise." Ouch. Or she could use this Gentle Start-Up instead: "I'm worried that there isn't enough money every month to cover our bills. I don't think they're paying you what you're really worth at work. How would you feel about asking for a raise?" Much better.

Now this one: Bert's been missing lovemaking with Sue. He wants them to make love tonight. Imagine how thrilled she'll be if he says, "Why are you so cold? You're about as hot as an iceberg."

A clever fellow in one of our workshops had the perfect Gentle Start-Up for this example. He said, "Honey, I'm horny tonight. I'm gonna go upstairs and have sex. Would you like to come along?" More or less, this guy had the right idea.

Contempt is the second Horseman of the Apocalypse. It's like criticism gone nuclear. It conveys insults, name-calling, put-downs, blame, and much more. Speakers don't just mumble about their partners' flaws; they declare them from on high. Contemptuous partners think they are superior. Their words are soaked with disgust and drip from their tongues like sulfuric acid. The effect is devastating.

Contempt is the most corrosive Horseman, without a doubt. It destroys not only relationships but also the listener's immune system. When John and his colleagues correlated the ways couples conflicted with later measurements of their health, they found that the number of times a partner expressed contempt during a 15-minute discussion predicted how many infectious illnesses the listening partner would get in the following four years. The more contempt, the more future infectious illnesses.

Ron and Jan Kiecolt-Glaser examined this phenomenon further. In their study they drew samples of blood moment by moment while couples discussed a conflict. Then they examined the blood droplets separately and noted what was happening in the discussion when each was taken. They found that when partners were listening to contempt, the strength and effectiveness of their lymphocytes, the engines of their immune system, declined precipitously. This drop in immune system power explained why the listeners in John's contemptuous couples were contracting so many infectious illnesses. They no longer had the immunity to ward them off. Contempt had destroyed it.

Contempt can be expressed verbally or nonverbally. Name-calling is one form of contempt, for example, calling someone a jerk, an idiot, an asshole. Contempt can also be expressed through sarcasm or mockery.

Let's look at some examples. Eve sneers and says sarcastically to Ray, "You're so caring and thoughtful; I'm sure you stopped and picked up the dry cleaning, right?" (when she knows he didn't). Or she pleads with Ray to drive more slowly, and he responds by mocking her and saying, "Oh Rayyyyy, oooooh, I'm soooo scared!" Contempt can also be delivered nonverbally.

When someone rolls their eyes or laterally pulls only the left corner of their mouth, creating a dimple, that's a cross-culturally universal facial expression contempt. When both are done together, that's a double whammy. Any of you with teenagers may catch these nonverbal signals from time to time. In his research, John found that contempt facial expressions are just as destructive as words.

The alternative to contempt that the masters of relationships employ is the same as with criticism: Gentle Start-Up. Most masters rarely if ever revert to contempt. If they do, it's a big deal. They know how destructive it is. So if it happens, they fall back on major repair efforts like the ones we described in Chapter 6 to reverse the damage.

If we return to the contemptuous remark Eve made to Ray about the laundry, here's a Gentle Start-Up she could say instead: "I'm disappointed that the dry cleaning wasn't picked up. Would you please pick it up tomorrow?" There's the feeling (disappointed), then what the feeling is about (that the dry cleaning hasn't been picked up), and finally, the positive request for how he can make her feel better. As for Ray's first reply to Eve's wanting him to slow down, instead of mocking her a great response would be, "okay," or perhaps, "I know I'm driving fast but I'm worried about getting there on time."

Which brings us to defensiveness, the Third Horsemen. Ray's contemptuous reply to Eve's driving request is also defensive. He's probably reading into her request that he's being criticized, so he mocks her as a counterattack. Defensiveness is a natural response to feeling unjustly blamed or attacked. In the moment, whether or not the speaker actually intends blame or attack is beside the point. What matters is what the listener hears. (Remember, there are always two points of view about what is happening in every interaction, and both have validity.) When partners think they are being attacked, they miss what may be their partner's plea for connection. They only hear disrespect or dislike or perhaps even hate and are likely to respond with defensiveness.

Our instinct for self-preservation underlies our defensiveness, so it's not surprising that defensiveness is so hard to banish. Since people aren't built to respond kindly to attacks, including verbal ones, they step back or hit back in order to protect themselves. There are two main types of defensiveness: (1) innocent victimhood, in which people claim they're being mistreated; or (2) righteously indignant counterattack, where they hurl criticism back at their partners in order to distract from their partner's complaints.

Here's a statement of innocent victimhood: "What about all the good I do in this relationship? I can never do enough to please you." (Imagine this being said in a whiney tone.)

And here's an indignant counterattack: "You're complaining about the dry cleaning again? Well, you're so lazy you never even go grocery shopping."

Neither of these replies leads to good problem solving. Instead they just fan the flames with more hot air.

The skill that replaces defensiveness may be the toughest to do. It is taking some responsibility for the problem at hand. Just a little bit can help. Phrases like, "Fair enough," or "Good point," can keep a conversation on the right track. For some people, however, words like these may feel too dangerous to say.

Partners may resist holding themselves accountable because they suffer from terrible self-esteem. If they are already full of self-loathing, they may believe that owning responsibility for a problem hands over evidence to their partner that they are, in fact, worthless. So they dig in their heels and loudly proclaim their innocence to deny their own culpability. I've had some partners say that when they acknowledge responsibility for a problem, they feel like they are stepping into a small crack in the Earth that turns out to actually be a deep crevasse. They find themselves hurtling down through the Earth's crust into a boiling lava core of self-hatred within. No wonder they ramp up their defensiveness at the slightest hint of blame.

But taking responsibility for mistakes or wrongdoing actually creates the opposite effect. After people acknowledge being wrong or making a mistake, their partners usually feel listened to and more respected and loved, which leads them to respect and love their humble mates even more. Acknowledging responsibility for a wrongdoing is like pouring water on the fire. It cools things down and soothes both speaker and listener. Then nobody gets burned.

Here are some examples of defensiveness and alternatives for it:

"Bill, stop interrupting me!"

DEFENSIVE RESPONSE: "I'm not interrupting you. You're just going on and on."

NONDEFENSIVE RESPONSE: "Sorry. I guess I was getting impatient."

"Lily, this place is a mess. You agreed to do the vacuuming, so when are you going to clean up all this dog hair?"

DEFENSIVE RESPONSE: "It's your dog. That dog sucks. I never wanted him. So you do it. Not me!" ("It's your dog" is a sideways counterattack that escalates the negativity.)

NONDEFENSIVE RESPONSE: "I'll try to get to it tonight. But can I say, it is amazing how much this dog sheds, isn't it?"

"We never make love anymore."

DEFENSIVE RESPONSE: "Yes we do. We just had sex last month."

NONDEFENSIVE RESPONSE: "I miss it, too. How about this weekend?"

As you can see, there are no bristles in a nondefensive response. Nondefensiveness smoothes ruffled feathers, maintains calm conflict management, and nurtures a peaceful partnership.

The fourth Horseman is stonewalling. Stonewalling is shutting down in the middle of a conflict discussion and withholding any verbal or nonverbal response to what's being said; in other words, acting like a stone wall in the middle of a discussion. John found that 85 percent of the heterosexual Stonewallers in his studies were men. When men stonewall during a conflict discussion, they typically fall silent, fold their arms, and look down or away for an extensive period of time. Women stonewall, too, especially ones who have endured physical, sexual, or emotional abuse during childhood. But women look different when stonewalling. They don't look away. They maintain eye contact with the speaker, but their eyes glaze over as if nobody's home. Their faces and bodies look frozen and lifeless, like a store window mannequin.

Through John's research we have learned that partners stonewall for good reason. When John matched up couples' physiological measures with their words and behavior during conflict discussions, he found that partners who stonewall are simultaneously in fight-or-flight, the common name for diffuse physiological arousal (DPA). Their hearts are racing at 100+ beats per minute, their breathing is rapid and shallow, and their bodies are perspiring, all while they sit quietly and converse. These changes are often impossible to observe with the naked eye, even if the observer is highly trained.

It's widely believed that DPA first evolved to empower our prehistoric ancestors to fight off life-threatening enemies like saber-toothed tigers. Only now, thousands of years later, the Stonewaller's big enemy is the saber-toothed wife sitting next to him. (Who knows? Maybe it was then, too.) DPA creates tunnel vision and tunnel hearing. For a Stonewaller in DPA, every one of his partner's expressions seems loud and red hot; they all signal, "Attack!" It's as if he has donned horror-film 3D glasses. Everything he experiences from his wife's direction looks dark and scary. She could be whispering romantic sonnets to him, but his DPA will contort the meaning of her words into yet more attack.

DPA diverts blood flow out of the brain's rational problem-solving centers, thus disempowering them, and redirects more flow to the brain's motoric centers. The process fuels fight-or-flight but leaves the Stonewaller ill equipped to think rationally. This is why the Stonewaller's attempts to solve problems usually fail.

As if this wasn't bad enough, DPA is also very physically

uncomfortable. The muscles tense up, including those in the gut, jaw, arms, and legs, and some people feel like they have ants under their skin. Unable to think straight or physically fight or flee, a Stonewaller in DPA withdraws from the couple interaction not to abandon or punish his partner but instead, to calm himself down. It's a bit like an overstimulated infant who instinctively turns his head away in order to reduce being further stimulated.

The skill that slows down DPA and prevents stonewalling is self-soothing. The trick is for partners to sense when DPA is first starting, before it has taken hold of their brain and body. Partners who are aware of their DPA report having a gauge, a signature response that signals DPA is hovering on the horizon. It may be a tightened gut, a clenched jaw, or shoulders shifting upwards. Others report first feeling hot, flushed, or shaky. An easy way to test for DPA is to take a quick pulse reading on the wrist or neck. When a person is accustomed to how their pulse normally feels, if their pulse rate seems unusually high mid-conversation, DPA is probably there, too, or at least, right around the corner.

When one partner feels emotionally flooded and is beginning to shift into DPA, he should immediately stop the discussion and tell the other partner he needs to take a break and what time he'll return to resume talking. Conversely, if the other person senses his partner's DPA is about to erupt, she can also call for a break. Once a break is requested, no one should try to get in the last word. That will only keep the pot boiling. Instead, they should agree on a time they'll return to talk and retreat to separate places where they won't see or hear their partner. Then it's time for self-soothing, especially for the partner in DPA.

For self-soothing to succeed, distracting and calming activities work best. Reading a book, listening to music, meditating, watching TV, practicing yoga, or taking a walk are all good choices. These facilitate a return to a more relaxed state. Ruminating about the fight or rehearsing future things to say will fail miserably; they sabotage self-soothing since they keep one mentally in the fray.

Breaks need to last at least 30 minutes but no longer than 24 hours. Otherwise waiting partners may end up feeling punished or abandoned. Once calmed down, both partners can return to talk together, now with DPA in check. With brain blood flow again enriching problem-solving centers, both partners can reengage in constructive conflict discussion and hopefully proceed towards peaceful resolution.

Now that we've reviewed healthier alternatives for conflict management, let's return to their clinical application. When fiery couples enter our office, it's our job to equip them with tools that can rein in the Four Horsemen and cool down their conflict management. This isn't easy. Sometimes we have to verbally wedge ourselves between the partners to interrupt their interaction, especially if they are chomping at the bit to attack each other. Once they pause, we need to spotlight their destructive pattern, explain why it isn't working if appropriate, boost the authority of what we're saying with research data, and teach the couple a more gentle way to speak to one another. Then we can back out again and let them return to their dialogue in hopes that they will employ their new skills. If they fail again, it may be time for them to put on pulse oximeters (small devices that clip onto the index finger to measure heart rate and oxygen saturation levels) to see if either one is flooded and in DPA. If a partner's pulse rate exceeds 100 beats per minute, that person is in DPA. Then we should stop the interaction and take 5–10 minutes to do a soothing exercise for both partners that helps them calm down. Afterward, they can resume their dialogue with a quick review of how to practice the new skills.

John and I have two favorite methods to convert couples who are stuck in attack-defend patterns to a calmer conflict management style. The first method is based on the work of Anatol Rapoport, a brilliant Russian immigrant who had originally trained as a concert pianist. After obtaining a PhD in mathematics, he moved into the field of social psychology, studied how to help people to be more cooperative, and applied what he learned to work on establishing international peace during the Cold War. He observed that diplomats couldn't listen to another's opposing position until they felt their own position had been validated first. John and I borrowed this insight and applied it to couples who were also on the brink of war in what we called the Gottman-Rapoport Exercise.

Here's how this method works: When partners want to discuss a specific conflict issue, they postpone persuasion until each one can summarize the other partner's position to their partner's satisfaction. First one partner begins as the speaker while the other listens. Let's say the Mrs. speaks first. Her job is to say what she needs regarding an issue without blame or criticism. She begins with a Gentle Start-Up and describes what she feels and what situation has evoked her feelings and then what she needs. Stating a positive need rather than a negative one works best, that is, what she *does* need, rather than what she *does not* need. (Incidentally, in this context we consider wants and needs interchangeable; they are both important.) Her partner's job as the listener is to take notes on what she says and only ask questions for clarification and understanding. It's crucial that he postpones bringing up his own point of view until it's his turn to speak.

After she finishes speaking, he summarizes her position, checking to make sure he's got it right. Here's where the notes help out. Then he does his best to stand in his partner's shoes and validate her position by saying words like, "From your point of view it makes sense to me that you need . . . " Or simply, "Okay, I get it. I understand." Once he validates her position, they exchange roles. Now he gets a turn to describe his position on the issue while his partner listens, takes notes, and then summarizes and validates what she has heard him say.

This method stops the stampede of the Four Horsemen as long as both speakers use Gentle Start-Up when stating their needs. A Gentle Start-Up short-circuits any criticism, blame, or contempt. And because listeners are busy taking notes, they're less likely to get defensive. They also know that it will soon be their turn to be listened to. Since attack and defensiveness are avoided and flooding and DPA are also rarely triggered, for the most part the Four Horsemen stop cavorting and take a rest.

Although this intervention usually succeeds, I wouldn't be honest without admitting that sometimes it flat-out fails, too. Here's a case in point. Bobby and Angela were in their 40s and had four kids, two of whom were teenagers. They had terrible arguments. Bobby worked as an executive. With his boyish face, thatch of hair, and lean athletic build, he was a charmer. Angela was a writer. She, too, was beautiful with high cheekbones and flashing green eyes. They had met in college, had a whirlwind affair, and married straight out of school.

Bobby grew up the youngest of four brothers. At 11, a tragedy derailed his life when his mother was struck by a hit-and-run drunk driver and thrown fifty feet down the road. In a coma for months, she eventually regained consciousness, but the vivacious woman was gone, reduced to the remains of a damaged brain and a wheelchair. She never mastered thinking beyond that of a six-year-old, and she never walked again. At the time, Bobby's brothers were in college or graduate school. Not long after Mom returned home, Dad divorced her and then three years later, remarried and moved out of state. Bobby was left alone to care for his mother.

Angela's early life was sweet compared to Bobby's. Her parents were successful entrepreneurs who grew their assets so rapidly that by the time Angela came along, the family had pole-vaulted from their working class beginnings to the socioeconomic stratosphere. When she was eight they moved to a large ranch, where Angela became quite a good Western equestrienne. By high school, she owned a fine Arabian horse and was competing nationally in barrel racing.

Bobby and Angela met in a college English class. Bobby was entranced by her cocky classroom comments and her proud, regal demeanor and pursued her with cards, gifts, wining and dining. She couldn't resist. Her parents weren't thrilled with her choice but soon fell under Bobby's charm, and the wedding was glorious.

After marrying, their kids came quickly. Meanwhile, Bobby joined a tech firm and rose swiftly through the ranks to a high executive position. Their paths diverged—hers, hovering over the kids, and his, chained to his cell phone and computer. Soon their arguments grew entrenched and over the years, rageful. Angela's debating style grew razor-edged and toxic, and occasionally Bobby punctuated his yelling with a shove or push. By the time they came to me, I was amazed they were both standing, so venomous were their fights. Intervention began with processing their past emotional injuries—huge battles they had never repaired afterwards. This took months. Finally they were ready to tackle their current conflicts and how they managed them.

One day they came in quarreling about buying an expensive horse for their daughter, who, true to her mother's blood, loved riding, too. Bobby was adamantly opposed to the idea. Angela angrily accused him of blocking their daughter's dream to ride well enough someday to compete at big shows. Here's what their discussion sounded like:

BOBBY: You're being ridiculous. She's 12 years old. What the hell does she need a $30,000 horse for? Just because you were spoiled doesn't mean you have to spoil our daughter.

ANGELA: How dare you? It's okay for you to spend thousands on old cars while you deprive your kids of what they need? What kind of father are you? You're just like your own father—a selfish, narcissistic bastard.

I interrupted. "Hold on, people. Let's pause for a minute. Do you think this conversation is working for you?"

Looking frustrated, they shook their heads.

"Okay, let's try something different. I'm hearing lots of criticism and contempt between you, put-downs and name-calling.

That will just make you both defensive. You both want to be listened to, but with words like these, that's not going to happen. It's impossible to listen when you feel attacked. Remember, research points to criticism and contempt as big predictors of relationship demise, right? So let's try something different. Let's slow things down and try a speaker-listener exercise to see if that helps. Are you okay with that?"

They nodded.

"Good. Here's what we'll do. One of you will be the speaker while the other is the listener." I went on to describe the roles of each. "Who wants to start as the speaker?"

Angela said, "I will."

ANGELA: I love our daughter. I want to support her dreams. That means buying her a high-quality horse that she can train and learn from, so someday she'll be good enough to compete. That's what she really wants. And I want us to support her by getting her a decent horse.

BOBBY: Why do we have to get her such an expensive one?

JULIE: Careful, Bobby, you're edging into your own point of view here. Just stay with questions to help you understand Angela's point of view for now.

BOBBY: What does a "decent horse" mean?

ANGELA: Probably either a pure-bred quarterhorse or an Arabian young enough to train but with good enough breeding lines to guarantee speed, agility, and a good temperament.

BOBBY: Help me get this. I don't understand why such a horse has to be so expensive.

ANGELA: Because that's what it takes. They're expensive. Why is it such a big deal to you? We have the money. It's not as if we're poor.

JULIE: Angela, you're slipping into your old debating style again. Can you try to explain your own point of view without alluding to Bobby's viewpoint?

BOBBY: Yeah, Angela.

ANGELA: Yeah, what? Just cuz you're such a cheapskate, you'd rather spend big bucks on yourself than your own daughter!

BOBBY: There you go again with the insults. I can't stand talking to you! This is hopeless!

JULIE: Okay, let's slow things down here. Angela, criticism sneaked in there again. Try taking a deep breath. That's right, another . . . one more . . . Okay. Do you want to try again? I think Bobby's question was about why horses like these cost so much.

ANGELA: How am I supposed to answer that? Because fine horses cost money. Period. We can get her a lousy horse, an old nag, and fine, she can ride that. But then you can just face her disappointment, because it'll be your fault.

BOBBY: I can't take this.

We went round and round like this. Every time they began this exercise and others designed for calmer talk, they would slip off the rails into angry critical confrontation. For the life of me, I couldn't stop it. We tried pulse oximeters, my voicing different words for them, every intervention I could think of, and nothing worked, at least not for long. I struggled with self-doubts, racked my brain for what I was missing, consulted others, and tore my hair out. I couldn't figure it out. We hung in there together, and at least they eliminated the physical fighting, the pushes and shoves, plus some of the more abusive wording. But I failed at radically changing their vicious conflict style. Finally, a new job for Bobby moved them out of state and out of therapy. Our work may have helped a little, but certainly not to the degree I hoped it would. I cared about this couple a great deal and felt miserable that I couldn't help them. At times like this it's clear that we know a fair amount about helping couples, but there's still so much more to learn.

This couple tended to spin into DPA within seconds of opening their mouths. No matter what they tried—yoga, biofeedback, meditation—nothing seemed to slow it down. DPA stepped into the office the minute they entered and wouldn't leave them be. As a result, calm conflict management proved impossible to achieve. It's interesting but sad how some individuals can be so intelligent, educated, and sophisticated and want a loving warm relationship, but their bodies will sabotage their every effort to have one. It's not their fault. It's not even their choice. Whether genetics, the intrauterine environment in which they gestated, or simple bad luck leads them to have unremitting DPA, they are stuck with it. There's no greater obstacle to a long-lasting happy relationship than DPA's relentless interference. Yet why should partners like this be deprived of the peaceful relationship refuge they long for? More research is needed to understand how we can better help them.

Soon after Bobby and Angela left treatment, another couple filled their time slot. What a difference. Both in their 70s and infinitely calmer, Lizzy and Rebecca had lived together for many years. Lizzy had married young, had three kids and raised them, but had been unhappy in her heterosexual relationship. After her last child had entered college, she left her husband and soon after joined a circle of lesbian artists, writers, and musicians. She felt like she'd come home.

Rebecca had never married, had always been attracted to women, but was terribly shy. After being raised with seven siblings, she had retreated into a mostly solitary life. She earned her living by editing textbooks. One evening she took a big risk and ventured out to one of the meetings of the circle. There, she was immediately drawn to Lizzy's belly-deep laugh and wild wit. Lizzy, in turn, admired Rebecca's quiet contemplative nature. After six months of dating, they joined households, then left the city hubbub for a broken-down farmhouse on an evergreen island. They were slowly repairing the place themselves as it became the sanctuary where they could live in peace.

Sadly, Lizzie's health deteriorated soon after she turned 68. A stroke left her partially paralyzed. Over several years she fought back and slowly recovered some of her upper-body movement, but the stroke had sapped much of her strength. Rebecca was now saddled with most of the housework and Lizzy's caretaking. Exhausted and frustrated, she grew ill-tempered and withdrawn. Lizzy didn't know what to do. They came into therapy, afraid they were losing their closeness.

Lizzy was as small and round as Rebecca was tall and angular. They both wore their white hair long and free. Lizzy draped herself in baggy dresses, while Rebecca dressed in plaid shirts with frayed edges and pants that stopped short of her ankles. Their eyes shone with sweetness. But Rebecca's face was gaunt and pale.

One day Rebecca came in disgruntled. She was angry and in the session accused Lizzy of using her disability as an excuse to not help out at home. She called Lizzy passive-aggressive. In response, Lizzy expressed dismay and deep hurt. It looked like these two could use a Gottman-Rapoport intervention to dismantle the criticism and help them state their underlying feelings and needs. After instructing them in the details of the exercise, here's what emerged:

REBECCA: Lizzy, I'm exhausted. I'm frustrated. I can't do all of this alone. Either we need to sell the farm and move back to a condo somewhere or you're going to have to do something.

JULIE: Rebecca, can you say more about what you're feeling and what you need? You're moving a little too fast into problem solving instead of stating what your need is.

REBECCA: I don't know how to say what I need. We were never taught to do that as kids. In fact, we were supposed to shut up, put up with what was going on, and just make do. With eight of us, there were too many of us to talk about needs. My poor mother had enough on her hands just getting food on the table.

JULIE: Yes, that makes sense. So going inside and taking care of yourself was your way of adapting to that. It was a good survival skill back then. But now you're not with seven other kids anymore. You're with your lover and best friend.

Try letting her in a little more. She may not be able to do all that you need, but I imagine she wants to at least hear what your needs are. Am I right, Lizzy?

LIZZY: Yes, definitely. If you don't tell me what you want, I have no idea what to do. Look, I really appreciate everything you've done for me, Bec, but I am getting stronger and I want to do more. Really. So just tell me. What's going on with you? What do you need?

REBECCA: Well, paying the bills would be a start. And if you can manage it, maybe filing your mail and papers to so they're not sprawled all over our kitchen table.

JULIE: Rebecca, can you say more about how you feel, too?

REBECCA: I'm sad. I'm sad all the time. I feel like I can't keep up with everything. I love our place. I love our life. But it's just so hard now. I tell myself just keep going. But sometimes I just can't. Sometimes I want to curl up and go to sleep and never wake up.

LIZZY: That scares me, Bec. What are you saying?

REBECCA: Oh, it's not so bad, I suppose. I'm just so tired that sometimes I don't know how to keep going. It feels like a no-win. If I keep up with everything, we can keep the place, but I end up a mess. If I ask for help, I'm bad for imposing on you and making you feel terrible that you can't do more. So endless sleep looks appealing. But I know I'm just being melodramatic.

JULIE: Rebecca, wait a minute. You've just described a pretty painful state. Sometimes you feel hopeless that you'll ever have your good life back. Or for that matter, your healthy partner. The changes you've both gone through are painful. There's been a lot of loss, not just for Lizzy, but for you, too. You have a right to your feelings. And it's okay to let Lizzy in on them.

REBECCA: Yeah, but I don't want to scare her.

JULIE: So check with her. See if she's still scared.

REBECCA: Are you?

LIZZY: No, not now. I *do* want to know what you feel. And what you need. I don't want you to feel sad or hopeless or this exhausted. I appreciate all you've done, but I know it's too much. You can't go on working this hard. How are we going to have sex if you're this tired?

REBECCA: Good point.

LIZZY: So go on, tell me.

REBECCA: Well, I'm tired. I'm frustrated. I feel hopeless that I can keep up with everything that needs to be done. I know you're doing your best, and you're working hard to get strong again. But I still need some help with whatever you can do. In fact, there's no way I can just keep going, doing it all myself. I really need more help from you. There, I said it.

From here, they talked more about what Rebecca needed. Once Lizzy had summarized and validated Rebecca's feelings, it was easier for them to figure out what small tasks Lizzy could accomplish that would lift some of the pressure from Rebecca's sagging shoulders. For a start, Lizzy agreed to take on the feeding of their two cats and dog, some of the light dusting, the filing for her papers, and taking on all the insurance claims regarding her medical care.

Therapy didn't take long. Aided by their calmer temperaments, they worked hard on shifting out of their prior attack-defend style and into a more productive openness about their feelings and needs. Their conversations began to flow smooth as cream.

A year after they finished therapy, I received an invitation to their wedding. After 30 years together, it was about time they could legally tie the knot.

Bringing It Into Practice

- The biggest predictors of poor conflict management and future relationship demise are criticism, contempt, defensiveness, and stonewalling.
- Individuals often shut down and stonewall when they are in diffuse physiological arousal.
- Teach couples how to take a break from a conflict discussion when they are in diffuse physiological arousal.
- The healthy alternative to criticism and contempt is Gentle Start-Up.
- The antidote to defensiveness is taking some responsibility for a problem.
- Conflict management works best when the partner who is listening understands and summarizes the other partner's point of view before bringing up his or her own.

THE EIGHTH PRINCIPLE
Strengthen Friendship and Intimacy

Earlier in my life (before turning 50), I loved to climb mountains. On my days off, I would crawl up glaciers and scramble up summits. I had to fight for every breath. When I made it, perching on top was glorious. Afterwards there was a delicious hot bath. I tried to not dwell on the harder challenge awaiting me the next day, the first couple on Mondays. Like the high peaks, they, too, were frigid. If I matched my breath to theirs, I grew short of oxygen in under five minutes. It was much like mountain climbing. I swear the room temperature dropped 20 degrees when they sat down.

Edward and Thelma were in their late 60s. They'd been married since they were both 21. He was a family physician who worked for an HMO. She was a freelance writer of articles for gardening magazines. Their only child, a daughter, was grown and long gone.

Both people were very shy. Edward had a red fuzzy pate and a pale complexion that burned pink with embarrassment whenever he was asked to speak. Thelma simply looked away most of the time, tight as a drum skin. Her pale eyes seemed perpetually sad.

Thelma had undergone psychoanalysis four times a week for the past six years to help her cope with unrelenting depression. Medications hadn't helped much, though perhaps the therapy couch had. She reported how she had laid down after her daughter left home and hadn't gotten up for a year. She had rarely opened the blinds.

With help from her psychiatrist, she eventually arose and created a little study for herself in the attic. She wrote her first articles there. She was overjoyed when one was accepted for publication. Her years working hard in the backyard had finally paid off. With her knowledge well received, she was renewed. Most of her time she now spent perusing new rose varieties at local nurseries.

Meanwhile Edward plugged away at his job. He had never been close to their daughter, so her leaving changed little for him. He did notice his wife's absence, but it didn't bother him much. They hadn't been close for a long time. Sex had disappeared long ago, and before that, it was a rare perfunctory blip on the screen. They had slept in separate bedrooms for 10 years. On his time off, Edward sang baritone in a church choir. He had a lovely voice.

They wanted therapy to make that final decision—either change the relationship or divorce. I wondered, why now? They were both aging, they said. Lately the distance between them had taken on a deeper sorrow and more aching loneliness. They weren't sure why. Maybe it had something to do with Thelma's increasing well-being as her psychoanalysis progressed. She no longer wanted to live with a ghost. Better that she live alone, feather her own nest the way she wanted to and enjoy real solitude rather than live with a phantom that hovered nearby, present but untouchable. That had worked for years, but no longer.

Edward was frightened. He didn't want to live alone. He felt too old to start over. If he could, he would rather stay with Thelma. He loved her once. He wasn't sure he could again. But why not try?

These two were the epitome of the emotionally distant couple. They had no cuddles together, no conversations together, no savoring meals together, no garden walks together, not even church together. Thelma never attended Edward's choir concerts, and Edward never read Thelma's published articles. In short, they lived together like strangers.

Where does one begin with a couple like this? Work on conflict management? No. It's not even on the radar screen. Work on sex? Obviously no. How about creating shared meaning? Hard to do when they have barely spoken to each other in years. Too deep, too fast.

It is time to focus on our eighth principle: strengthen friendship and intimacy.

This couple was barely breathing, yet alone reaching out to one another. It had been so long since they had actually enjoyed time together, they barely remembered each other's names. The methods John and I had created to strengthen friendship and intimacy perhaps could help them.

In the late 1980s John was generously granted some additional research space at the University of Washington, where he built the apartment lab (described in Chapter 1). In a study of newlyweds, couples packed up clothes, books, drinks, and food and planted themselves in the apartment lab for a stay of 24 hours. Except for bedtime hours, their every move, word, and heartbeat was videotaped and measured. When John and his colleagues reviewed thousands of hours of tape from this study, they saw tremendous differences between happy and unhappy couples that, as it turned out, were highly predictive of happy and successful versus broken and unsuccessful relationships in the future. Happy couples turned towards each other most of the time, responding with interest and warmth to their partners' bids for connection. Unhappy couples turned away or against their partners' bids, either ignoring them or responding to them with hostility. Happy couples asked each other personal questions to deepen their knowledge of one another. Unhappy couples avoided asking questions and instead focused only on broadcasting their own points of view. Happy couples made sure to highlight their time together with rituals of connection, sweet and predictable shared moments like holding hands and saying grace before dinner. Unhappy couples shared no such times. They floated through space like disconnected, isolated asteroids with no gravitational pull linking them together.

We knew from the results of this study that working on conflict management wouldn't be enough to repair and restore all broken relationships. We also had to create therapy methods that deepened a couple's friendship and intimacy. In addition, from John's earlier studies we knew there were two peak times when fragile couples ended up separating. The first peak, sometime around year three post-wedding, was marked by relationships ending with a bang. Couples who separated this early typically suffered from terrible conflict management. But the second peak, around year 15, consisted of couples whose relationships ended with a sigh. Over the years, these couples had slowly grown emotionally distant and disconnected. It was this second group that especially needed to recharge their friendship and intimacy.

We designed a dozen methods to help draw these partners together again. A few focused on merely reacquainting them with each other. Others prompted them to move closer still. One of our favorites involved a discussion in which they selected open-ended questions to ask each other that explored deeper layers, like how their partner had evolved over time. These methods helped couples to update their Love Maps of one another and learn who their partner was now.

William Doherty's work also proved pivotal to our efforts to strengthen couples' friendship. Doherty (1999) wrote a wonderful book called *The Intentional Family*. In his research he found that relationships remained strong when couples practiced rituals of connection, regular and predictable ways of connecting that they could count on. The rituals could be as brief as a quick hug and kiss before parting every morning, or as grand as an annual holiday excursion. Dinners, date nights, reunions at the end of the day, birthday celebrations, holiday festivities, bubble baths together—any and all could be crafted into rituals of connection by couples making intentional their ways of honoring these moments in time.

We liked Doherty's insights about the importance of rituals of connection and integrated his idea into our collection of friendship-strengthening methods. We thought it would prove especially helpful for couples who had lost all routines of connecting except for the occasional list checking like, "Did you call the plumber?"

With these methods in mind, I approached my work with Edward and Thelma. I hoped to help the couple build a bridge that could arc over the chasm between them. First some scaffolding was needed—simple facts about one another. It had been years since they had asked each other any light questions, let alone explored what was on each other's minds and hearts. They had never shared how they had each changed over their four decades together. In some ways they were like strangers sharing a house who were bound together only by ancient memories, ones they never talked about. They needed to meet again, learn about each other again, and court again. If all went well, they could then build a bridge to one another with new rituals of connection, ones that were strong and lasting like brick rather than shifting sand.

In our first intervention session, I introduced them to a simple card game John and I had invented called the Love Maps Card Deck. The purpose of the game is to explore how much one partner knows about who the other partner is here and now—their preferences, needs, likes, and dislikes. It also helps them learn more about each other, so that by the end of the game, they can each accurately draw an updated map of their partner's inner world. Here's how it works:

Each card poses a simple question about a partner. The couple takes turns picking up a card. The first partner with a card reads the question on it out loud and tries to answer it in terms of the other partner's world. If he gets it right, hooray. If he doesn't, the other partner gently corrects him and gives him the right answer. Then it's the second partner's turn to pick up the next card, read it aloud, and guess at the right answer for the first partner. Nobody keeps score. The spirit of this game is simple fun. For example, if John and I were playing and he picked a card that asked, "What is your partner's favorite tree?" he might guess, "A Sequoia," because he knows I love these giants dearly. However, if I picked one that asked, "Who are your partner's best friends?" and then I guessed "Bob and Neil," he might say, "No, dear. Neil died three years ago. My other best friend now is Phil." (So much for a busy work schedule. Everybody needs occasional Love Map updates.)

Edward and Thelma knew many of the answers when they pertained to early historical information, like "Who was your favorite relative as a child?" But the present time questions, they colossally flunked. Edward had no idea who Thelma's friends were, nor the names of her favorite novel, favorite movie, favorite meal, or favorite flower. Thelma didn't fare much better. She couldn't name Edward's current colleagues, what part of his job he liked best, his favorite food, or his favorite composer. Despite their mistakes in guesswork, they seemed to enjoy the game. They even made eye contact and smiled once or twice. This showed improvement. This couple needed a light touch with which to begin therapy. Nothing too much. At this point their friendship was too atrophied to handle heavy lifting. The good news was that they wanted to keep coming back for more. They were beginning to construct some scaffolding: the new facts they had learned about each other.

A few sessions later we went deeper. I pulled out another one of our card decks, the Open-Ended Questions Card Deck. For these cards, the questions didn't have simple one-word answers. Instead they asked questions that needed longer and bigger answers, for example, "What dream would you like to fulfill in the next three years?" This time partners were not expected to know the right answers. They had a choice as to what depths they wanted to plumb with their partner and could ask a specific question accordingly.

Thelma and Edward cut the deck in half, then from their half they each picked one card with a question they wanted their partner to answer. After asking that question, their partner did their best to answer it. At first they hopped from question to question like rabbits running for cover. But soon long pauses began to precede their answers. They hadn't asked *themselves* such questions in years and needed time to summon their answers. They thought hard about ones like these: "What special qualities of your partner do you see in your child?" "What is the most important value you want your child to live by?" "What beliefs or values do you think are the most important ones to live by?" After several rounds, they found themselves speaking for much longer. Their answers took on more color and depth as they relaxed into shared reflections. They were learning much more about one other, and the foundational bricks were being set.

Next we tackled the art of conversation: how to start one, when to have it, and what to talk about. They needed new Rituals of Connection, ways of connecting with one another that they yearned for, had carefully designed, and could count on. But we had to be cautious. New scaffolding and a few bricks had begun to bridge the distance between them. But the framework was still fragile and if too top heavy, could topple over. Spending multiple hours together during a date night or sharing a weekend away were still a long way off. Jumping into these too soon might scare the dickens out of both partners.

They decided their first ritual would be sharing dinner together, something they hadn't done in more than 10 years. Thelma would cook. They decided on a realistic time they could eat together, given Edward's late work hours. Three times a week was plenty to begin with. Thelma needed to ask Edward his food preferences since her knowledge was outdated. To her surprise, over the past decade he'd developed a preference for vegetarian dishes. She would have to buy new cookbooks. But now the hard part: What would they talk about?

We generated a series of more tailored open-ended questions they could ask each other. There were some obvious ones: What were the highlights of your day? Were there any lowlights? If so, what were they? Then we added more: For Edward, what kind of medical problems did you have to deal with for your patients? What was the most challenging problem you encountered today? What music are you working on these days? Tell me about your favorite composition. And for Thelma: What kind of garden issues did you write about? Was there a special flower or plant you saw today? What made it special? What improvements would you like to make in our garden? These topics added a few more bricks to span the distance between them, so they weren't so frightened of the silence that had weighed down and collapsed their efforts earlier.

That was enough for now. After dinner they would do the

dishes together and could then retire to their separate corners of the house. The first week, they managed just one dinner time together. Good enough, I told them. It's hard to take the first steps. They're precarious. I congratulated them on having the courage to try something new. They pooh-poohed away the compliment. It was only 20 minutes, tops. Right, I said, but 20 minutes they hadn't done in years. I mentioned how many times I had seen couples in cafés sitting and blankly staring at walls, chewing their food like cud, saying nothing, then leaving with not a word spoken between them. They had once been a couple like that. But now they were talking, even if briefly—in my book, a breakthrough.

Slowly their dinner times increased in number and length. After two months they ventured out to try a new restaurant. Gradually movies, plays, and concerts followed. They began to relax and enjoy each other.

Then catastrophe hit. Thelma found in Edward's closet a gym bag full of women's lingerie. It wasn't hers. She confronted Edward about having an affair. He shook his head sadly. "Those are mine," he admitted.

Slowly Edward told her that every three or four months, when alone at home, he liked to dress up in women's underwear and stare at himself in the mirror. He had no idea why. He found it pleasing. In fact, it was a turn-on. He often masturbated while doing so. It had gone on for years. No, he wasn't homosexual. No, he wasn't yearning to change gender. Yes, he had practiced this during their entire marriage, even before they were married. Sometimes more often, sometimes less, depending on how stressed he was. The more stress, the more he did it. Call it a quirk. Why hadn't he ever told her? Too much shame. Too much guilt.

Thelma was dismayed and deeply threatened. I could feel their bridge starting to crumble from the aftershocks of this revelation. She said, "Maybe we should just separate and be done with it," words she hadn't spoken since their first assessment session. I cautioned her to wait a bit and let the dust settle before making any big decisions. Thelma decided to meet again with her analyst and asked me to inform her beforehand about what had transpired. Edward supported the idea and gave me his permission to speak with her. In a phone call later, the analyst immediately understood this was a crisis and we commiserated together.

The couple showed up for their next session pale and silent. Thelma expressed her pain and confusion. Edward just shook his head. She cried, clearly at a loss of how to move forward. She said, "I just don't know how to understand this."

"Thelma," I said. "Sex is a mystery. There is so little we understand about it. We've just started to comprehend its biochemistry. But the way it's expressed? Freud used to call it 'polymorphous perversity.' He liked to pathologize everything that wasn't straightforward, heterosexual intercourse. But now we know differently. We understand that healthy sexuality takes all kinds of forms. Every culture encompasses a broad spectrum of sexual behavior. As long as no one is being forcefully injured, the rest is part of our individual self-expression. It's like colors of the rainbow. There are millions of different hues out there, none any better than another. We don't judge red because it's not blue, or gray because it's not pure enough to be black. Color just is. Sexuality is like that, too."

Now I was speaking to both of them, trying to dissolve some of Edward's shame. "Is Edward doing any real harm in dressing in women's clothing? No, he isn't. It's something he does in private, something that gives him pleasure. It doesn't fit everybody's sexuality. But it fits his. The fact that he masturbates during it is quite common, too. Did you know that men actually masturbate more when they're married than when they're single? A little known fact. And they masturbate to all kinds of stimuli. Some like porn, some like erotic literature, some like sadomasochistic fantasies, some like visualizing women, some like visualizing men, some like imagining they're leopards. You never know, with humans. We can be very creative. Edward manifests one aspect of his sexuality in this particular way. There's nothing sick or weird in it. It's just his special way of being human."

"Is this why we stopped having sex? Because he preferred this over me?"

Edward burst out, "No, Thelma. It was never that. You didn't want sex. You kept saying, 'No.' Or being too tired. Or too something. And we were so distant anyway, it was easier to stop asking. But I've always desired you, Thelma. I just didn't think I could have you."

"Oh," Thelma said. "Well, I suppose you're right. I haven't been interested for a long time, I know. Especially after menopause. And that was a long time ago. But this dressing up, it scares me."

"Why?" Edward asked.

"Because it's so different. I don't know. I was not raised with such things. I don't know what to make of it."

"Thelma?" I gently asked. "Don't you think that if Edward practiced this privately from time to time just as he always has, without telling you if you preferred that, that you could stretch yourself a little more and try to accept it as part of who he is, as simply another aspect of him like his beautiful singing or his sensitive skill with patients? That it's just another manifestation of the gentler, more creative, and perhaps more feminine side that renders him so sensitive in the first place?"

"Well, I'd like to. But I don't know. I'll have to think about it."

"Fair enough."

After a moment, Edward said, "And getting back to sex? You know, I still do miss it. But now not as much as before. I guess getting older helps. But I wish we could have some kind of touch. Especially at night. I get really lonely at night."

Thelma replied, "Well, I can't sleep with you. You snore too much."

"I know."

"This is all so much to take in . . ."

They paused.

Thelma said, "I never want to have sex again."

"I know. I accept that."

"And I never want to see that gym bag again."

"Yes. Okay."

"I never want to hear about this again."

He sighed. "Yes, I understand. . . . Do you think you'll ever want any kind of touch with me?"

"Maybe. I don't know. I'll need some time to recover from all this." Then, "But I miss it, too."

"You do?"

"Yes."

"What about a few minutes of cuddling?" I asked. "Nothing much, just a hug or two. Is that something you might like, either one of you?"

Edward picked up on it. "That would be nice. It might even help me get to sleep. I don't sleep very well."

Thelma said, "You don't? Hmm." She paused. "Maybe we could try it once, just a little . . . before you go to sleep. But I'd want to get up. I always stay up later than you. You know I'm a night owl."

"And I have to get up early to go to work. But maybe just one hug before I go to sleep?"

"Maybe. I guess we could try that."

For now, the bridge stopped shaking and grew still. Much more work was needed. We hadn't even touched conflict management yet. Despite Edward's admonitions that he rarely wanted sex these days, he did. And Thelma didn't. This was their first big problem to solve together. It took a month to work through it. As hard as it was for her to accept his occasional transvestism, he had to accept her limitations, too. Sex was out of the question. Could he be satisfied with only cuddling with Thelma while resorting to sex with only himself?

Fortunately, as he stared down turning 70, the answer was, "yes."

Bringing It Into Practice

- Work on strengthening friendship and intimacy with emotionally distant couples.

- Help couples to create rituals of connection—ways of being together that are predictable and comforting.
- Remind partners to ask each other open-ended questions to maintain emotional intimacy.
- Strong friendship is the key to passion and good sex.

9

THE NINTH PRINCIPLE

Suspend Moral Judgment When Treating Affairs

Since the Ten Commandments first appeared many centuries ago, people have condemned husbands and wives with wandering hands and eyes who have had extramarital affairs. Judges, clerics, and townspeople have stoned women, drawn and quartered men, or exiled both for love outside of marriage. In some places affairs are still legally punishable today. Yet affairs haven't disappeared. They still strain marriages. The percentage of married men having affairs ranges from 18 to 45 percent. Now that more women work outside the home and have access to other partners, the number of women with affairs is growing, too. More recently the Internet has enabled millions to have affairs. Websites openly introduce roaming spouses to each other. Newspapers advertise meet-up spots for adulterers looking for new partners. There's no doubt, affairs are easier to set up than ever. Yet they tax marriages to the breaking point. Although affairs are less likely to split up couples than factors like long-term hostility, the amount of sheer pain they cause is daunting.

Therapists often fear treating couples with affairs. Nothing will flood budding counselors more than the words, "He (she) betrayed me." Couples are frequently told, "We won't be talking about the affair now." Or "You must forgive and move on." These are terrible words for betrayed partners to hear. How can they move on when nightly dreams feature their partners fornicating with that Other? In the worst-case scenarios, partners who have done the betraying face stern, disapproving glances from their therapist. Their partners shower them with contempt, and their counselors subtly endorse that contempt.

To be fair, we therapists face a dilemma. We witness the devastation affairs cause not only to partners but to their children as well. We know that affairs result from choices affair partners make. They don't happen due to the randomness of fate. Yet we are admonished to not take sides.

Crucial to our understanding is that affairs don't usually begin in a vacuum. When John examined the data of hundreds of couples with affairs, he discovered no less than 24 precursor steps that lead up to and predicted future betrayal.

John's careful analysis of affair-riddled couples revealed that they often start out happy and in love. But over time, poor conflict management skills take a toll. Either their fights grow ugly, or there is no fighting at all. Eventually both patterns lead them to shut down and avoid discussing disagreements altogether. After a while they shun any honest conversation and each other. Gradually they descend into canyons of loneliness. Just when they feel the worst after falling down to the canyon floor, they discover a lovely flowing river: a sweet young woman at the office. A sympathetic listener in the cubicle next door. The guy they keep running into at the gym. Before long there's an Other, the one who listens, the one who laughs, the one who sympathizes, the one who brings fresh croissants every morning. Soon they are swept up by the waves of romance. They begin to compare their current mate with the Other. Blinded by the Other's brilliance and beauty, the mate is left far behind in the dust. Rushing downstream, they plunge headlong over the waterfall and into an affair.

Caryl Rusbult, a brilliant psychologist, identified this process of unhappy mates making comparisons. She called it CL-ALT, or comparison level with alternative relationships. She observed plenty of unhappy couples out there. But not all of them took this additional step of negatively comparing their mates to other potential partners, thus living by the proverbial phrase, "The grass is always greener . . ." She found it was this final step that plunges couples into the tumult of betrayal.

Shirley Glass was another brilliant psychologist. She specialized in treating affair-ridden couples, crafting a therapy full of compassionate insight that guided them slowly back to each other. First, she understood that betrayed partners almost always suffer from Posttraumatic Stress Disorder (PTSD). They are much like soldiers returning from war. Traumatized vets live on high alert, looking for enemies behind every tree. So do betrayed spouses. Hypervigilance rules their every waking hour. Secretly they pour over their partner's phone records, email messages, texts and receipts, looking for the signs of midnight trysts. Combat vets suffer from flashbacks. So do betrayed partners. Feverishly they have visions of their spouse in bed with the Other. Neither vets nor betrayed partners can stop the images from invading their thoughts. Both are buffeted by waves of emotion: rage, pain, panic, and numbness that sink them into depression. Both suffer from insomnia and nightmares. In short, they are hijacked by their symptoms. Neither vets nor betrayed partners can easily control themselves. They're at the mercy of their PTSD.

No wonder we hear partners who have had affairs say they feel like they're married to a cyclone now. No matter how many times they apologize, their partners don't stop the attacks, the incriminations, the incessant interrogations. PTSD has moved in with them.

Glass also understood a fundamental shift in marital dynamics that precipitates affairs. Ordinarily, married partners keep a window wide open between them through which they exchange confidences, daily updates, and the occasional complaint. Intimacy is nourished by the ground they share. They also build a wall around their couplehood that keeps others outside their sacred marital land.

But affair-prone partners follow a different course. At a certain point they stop confiding in each other, stop sharing daily stories, and stop raising their complaints about the relationship in order to keep it strong. In effect, they close their marital window and replace it with a wall. Then, when a friendly soul appears, one of the spouses begins an exchange. At first it's easy storytelling or joking around. But soon enough it's deeper confiding and complaining about the marriage, the same complaints they've withheld from their spouse. In effect, they open a window between themselves and the Other, just a crack at first but wider with time. Eventually, the windows and walls become reversed, with a wall of secrecy between the spouses and an open window between the betraying spouse and the Other. Glass describes this process in her brilliant book, *Not Just Friends* (Glass and Staeheli, 2004).

The work of Glass and Rusbult supports John's analyses of affairs and what causes them. Contrary to what many believe, it's not immorality or a weakness in character. It's not untamed lust or wanton temptation. Affairs are caused by an erosion of marital trust that begins long before major betrayal. The breakdown of trust starts with little ways partners turn away from one another; the appreciations that are silenced rather than spoken; the critical views of the spouse that take hold; and the negative comparisons with others that follow—these infect and eventually destroy intimacy.

Thus we arrive at our ninth principle for effective couples therapy: Suspend moral judgment when treating affairs.

In place of negative judgments, we need to provide an unbiased approach that compassionately serves both partners as they struggle to rebuild a collapsed marriage. Based on the insights of Glass, the research of Rusbult, John's in-depth analyses, and the Sound Relationship House theory, we have developed a specialized treatment for couples with affairs. It is composed of three phases: Atonement, Attunement, and Attachment. (John's two recent books, *What Makes Love Last*, Gottman and Silver, 2012; and Gottman, 2011; describe this treatment in detail.)

Let's review some basics of the first phase, Atonement, which is often the most difficult for couples to navigate. We find that betrayed partners only conquer their PTSD and begin to rebuild trust if they are allowed to ask the partner who's had the affair questions about the affair that the betrayer answers honestly.

His or her transparency is crucial. Also, any defensiveness on his or her part needs to be checked at the door. Defensiveness will only spoil any efforts to reconcile and incite greater rage from the betrayed partner.

But there are some questions the betrayed partner should avoid asking. Any details about the sex between the betrayer and the affair partner need to be tabled, since those details may feed the betrayed partner's visual imagination and thereby worsen his or her PTSD. All other questions are fair game.

Here are some examples of what is commonly asked: When did you first meet (the affair partner)? How did you meet? What did you talk about? When did you decide to make it a physical relationship? Did you take her (him) to . . . (some specific place)? Do any of our friends know? Who? How did they find out? What attracted you to him (her)? Did you love him (her)? Do you still? When did you know you were in love? How often did you meet? When you were gone that weekend, were you with him (her)? Where did you go? Do people at the office know? Why didn't you tell me? Do you still have feelings for him (her)? When did you last see or talk to him (her)? Have you broken up? When? How did you break up? Why do you want us to be together now? Why do you want me and not him (her)? This last question is often voiced in many different iterations.

In response to what is shared, the therapist supports the betrayed spouse to express his or her emotions directly to the other partner, but again there need to be limits on how this is done. Because the betrayed partner is deeply hurt, furious, and frightened, contempt and criticism are usually his or her first words of choice. The betrayed partner's flooding may cause big blow-ups, too. But like any other listening partner, the betrayer won't be able to rise above an avalanche of attack. So the therapist must help the speaker understand that criticism and contempt will only sabotage their being listened to. The therapist can give the speaker emotion-focused words to substitute for words of attack, such as "I'm so enraged . . . or anguished, hurt, devastated, destroyed, desolate." In response, the listener needs to express remorse; the more, the better. Apologies may need to be made over and over again, as for some time, the betrayed partner won't believe them.

While modifying how the betrayed partner speaks to their mate, it's also crucial that the therapist empathize with the betrayer. It's terribly difficult for the betrayer to listen to the intense emotions of the betrayed partner. It may feel like they're facing a firing squad every week. So they need just as much support as the betrayed partner, and sometimes even more. Simple words like, "This must be so hard to hear," can help. This Atonement phase may take weeks or even months to complete.

An important human dynamic underlies the Atonement phase that we described in Chapter 6: Apologies don't work if the recipient of the apology doesn't feel listened to and understood first. Apologies fail because they are spoken prematurely, before the betrayed partner has described their pain and felt understood. The betrayer needs to grasp how deeply their partner has been injured and then apologize for the specific wounds he or she has caused. Otherwise, their apologies will sound glib and insincere.

Phase Two or the Attunement phase can only begin after the betrayed partner has exhausted their list of questions and has nothing further to ask. In addition, the betrayed partner needs to have heard the betrayer's remorse and begun to take it in and believe it.

In Phase Two, the problems in the marriage now become the focus of therapy. Often it's the betrayed partner who signals that they're ready for a transition by hinting that his or her behavior during the marriage wasn't so perfect either. The betrayed partner may allude to times in the past when they remember saying mean things, shutting out their partner with icy silence, and so on. There's a subtle acknowledgment that it takes two to tangle up a marriage.

In the beginning of Phase Two, the partners often describe how somehow a cold desert sprung up between them that they didn't know how to fix and it left both of them feeling desolate and lonely. Trust slowly eroded, and the relationship became less and less safe. Intimacy, both emotional and physical, eventually vanished. Finally came the affair, which was the worst blow of all.

At this point, it's best for the therapist to clearly state that which is obvious: The entire process has indeed destroyed Marriage # 1. However, the relationship can still survive by creating Marriage # 2, in which the partners remain the same but the dynamics between them change.

From here on out, therapy puts the couple's relationship dynamics under a microscope. Every level of the Sound Relationship House is examined, and most get rebuilt. There may be past regrettable incidents in which the betrayer was left emotionally injured that need to be processed. There are almost always new conflict management skills that need to be learned and practiced. Perpetual gridlocked issues may need to be explored and underlying dreams brought to the surface. Love Maps must be updated, and each partner's needs must be clearly expressed and responses shared.

Expressing fondness and admiration inevitably requires many hours of work, especially for the betrayed partner. There is often a significant imbalance between how much fondness the betrayer must voice versus that of the betrayed partner, at least at first. A person's voicing love naturally draws them closer to the object of their love, which in turn opens them up to being hurt again—a step the betrayed partner is reluctant to take until more trust is established. It's typical to see a betrayed partner first admit to still loving their partner and then the next week, report either a relapse in their PTSD symptoms or a bad fight. In fact, as this phase unfolds it's often two steps forward, then one step back or sometimes three steps back as the couple slowly reshapes their relationship.

Finally along the way, individual issues may also need attention and work. After an affair is discovered, feelings of rejection, abandonment, and inferiority are pervasive, as well as guilt, shame, and humiliation—all may be leftovers from less than perfect childhoods, too. It solidifies the gains couples make to help each partner separate out the historical sources for such feelings from their more recent causes so the relationship isn't asked to carry more weight than it can bear.

Throughout every step of Phase Two, partners are taught to attune to each other. They are often asked to summarize each other's responses to ensure they clearly understand each other, to step into each other's shoes so they can fully empathize with each other's feelings, and to work on validating each other's points of view.

Once the couple shows significant improvement in their conflict management, know each other far better again, and regularly share new ways of connecting, the therapy can safely transition into Phase Three, Attachment. This is the phase in which a return to physical intimacy is most often addressed, although occasionally some betrayed partners will be sexual early on if they think it will help them hold on to their partner and not get rejected. Most betrayed partners need lots of time to rebuild their trust in the relationship first before risking the extreme vulnerability of sexual intimacy.

This is a good time for the couple to discuss their sexual preferences, the nuances that would make their erotic life more fulfilling. Of course, this discussion often triggers a backwards slide into questions about the betrayer's love life with the affair partner. It's important to gently refocus the couple back to their own relationship. They can create their own unique world now, one finely tuned to who they are as individuals and together. They may need to talk about how they would prefer sex to be initiated and how they can say no to sex without hurting the other partner's feelings. A romantic getaway may provide the couple with the time and privacy they need to renew their sexual life without the pressures of their day-to-day schedules.

Another step in Phase Three is to discuss what the consequence will be for any future betrayal. This is not a pleasant subject to discuss, but it's an important one. Most partners who have been betrayed already have this formulated, and if it hasn't been expressed yet, it lies in wait just under the surface. It's better for the partner to intentionally state the consequence clearly than have it erupt during some future battle at home.

Once these three phases have been completed, the therapy can safely come to an end.

Let's discuss a case. John and I were once approached together to treat a famous husband and his wife, Walter and June. Walter's work took him all over the world. At each place he was treated like a god. Women threw themselves at him. And in turn, he obliged them. By the time he and his wife came for therapy, he'd had more than 50 affairs in just under 15 years, and those were the ones he still could remember. June had confronted him many times, and each time he angrily denied her accusations. Finally she accumulated enough proof that he could no longer insist on his innocence. As June packed up their three young children to leave him, Walter begged her to stay and to try to work it out. She relented. That brought the couple to our door.

John and I met with them for what we call Marathon Therapy, which was designed by one of our senior Gottman-certified therapists, Andy Greendorfer. In this form of treatment, we work for three to four consecutive days, five to six hours a day. The intensity jet-propels the work as one intervention builds to the next. Couples can make great progress with this method.

When John and I work together, we each have a role. John's role is to give structured exercises to strengthen the relationship and to stay more present-focused; his wonderful sense of humor balances out the seriousness of the work. My role is to explore past traumas or themes that have hidden underground for decades but may still influence what's going on here and now. An advantage we have from being married and working together for so long is that our minds often work in sync. The result is that we often seem to think of the same thing in the same moment.

When our ideas differ, we like to openly discuss them in front of the couple as a way to role model the give-and-take of accepting influence from one another. On our best days, our work together is a dance.

Walter and June arrived on time. Walter towered over June. His huge frame filled up the doorway. Raised on a farm where he had physically worked hard his whole childhood, he had the muscles to show for it. He had grown up in the middle of a pack of five brothers. Theirs was a rough-and-tumble life. When not working, they roamed nearby forests together and settled their disputes with wrestling rather than words. Mom and Dad laughed at their antics, wiped their bloody noses, and sent them back outside. When they were defiant or disobedient, Dad doled out punishment swiftly and physically with a belt or fist, and then life went on. There was no time for coddling, crying, or clever words.

June was petite, fair, and soft-spoken. She had grown up in warmer climes where all was lush and languorous. The eldest of four, she helped her mother with the younger siblings and had a deeply nurturing soul. She met Walter at age 18. Their romance swept her heavenward. She married him two years later. June traveled everywhere with Walter as his fame skyrocketed. At 21, she bore their first child, a daughter, and three years later, twin sons. Now staying home, June cared for the kids and the three homes they quickly acquired. But without her wifely presence, Walter was swarmed by female admirers. Soon he succumbed to their charms. In late-night hours, sex was free and unfettered. Although he missed June and his kids greatly, his after-hours play dulled the edge of his loneliness.

One young woman showed up in city after city, apparently following him on the road. She was smart, beautiful, and enchanting. He fell in love with her, or at least in lust with her. Now they planned out every rendezvous.

Eventually Walter returned home for a hiatus. But the woman followed him there, too. Soon he was sneaking out most nights and meeting her on street corners, in all-night cafés, and down hidden alleys. He excused his absences by telling June he couldn't sleep and went out for walks to think. At first she believed him. Then she didn't. It didn't add up, all these late-night jaunts. One night she called a friend to watch the kids and followed him. The pain at seeing him embracing the woman emotionally eviscerated her. Barely able to stand upright, she limped home.

The next day the packing began. Walter was frantic. He didn't want to lose her or his beloved kids. Seeing the suitcases on the bed was like his father's fist in his face. He woke up.

As Walter recounted this episode to us, he covered his face and sobbed. The tears were real, not there for show, though we weren't sure at first. June looked on, impassive and unimpressed. We explained what treatment would entail. In Phase One of treatment, the questions June asked Walter might feel like a Gestapo interrogation. He had to answer them absolutely honestly, and they might take up much of our time together. June would also be encouraged to express her feelings, although how she worded them would be shaped by us if need be. We would do our best to support Walter as well as June throughout the process. We were not here to judge or sentence him. Our job was to help them understand the truth of what had happened to them, both individually and together. Then, if they both wished it, in Phases Two and Three, we would give them new ways to be together, ones that would hopefully replace the faulty ways they had communicated in the past.

We explained to them that June was suffering from PTSD as a result of Walter's affairs. This became obvious during her individual assessment interview. While she may have suspected infidelity earlier, learning the truth of it was an unpredictable blow, a terrible shock to her system. She had been like somebody walking across a field full of landmines. She hoped she wouldn't step on one, but then she did. Now she was suffering the results of that explosion, including unwanted, intrusive pictures in her head of Walter with other women, the need to be hypervigilant, times when she felt numb, and times when she was swept away by attacks of panic or rage. In the coming months these symptoms would probably recede. But from time to time, if triggered they could return at any time.

We doubted that we could complete all the work they required during this marathon. They would need to do follow-up work, either with us or another therapist. At that point we didn't know what their outcome would be. Although Walter was sure he wanted the marriage, June remained dubious and leaned more towards ending it. The outcome would depend in part on Walter's transparency and honesty, how remorseful he really was, and how committed they were to change.

They acknowledged our words. Then we opened up the floor for June's questions. The first one was a whopper: "Name all the women you've slept with, and if you can't name them, count them."

Walter began. His answer took 20 minutes to verbally download. June wrote down every name plus marks for the unnamed. Fifty-seven in all.

"How many did you fall in love with? Which ones?"

Walter stuttered, "Umm, uhh, three. Uhh, Lisa, Jenny . . . and Melissa."

"I knew it," June said sadly. "Melissa. I saw you with her once at a party and I could tell there was more to it than flirting. But you lied. You said there was nothing between you." Then she erupted, "How could you? God damn you, you fucking bastard!"

"I'm so sorry, June. I know. I *am* a bastard. It was all wrong. I'm a shit!" Again, he sobbed.

June just looked at him. This time she cocked a brow, looking quizzical.

"I don't know what to believe," she said. "How do I know you're not just faking it to get us all back?"

"I'm not!" he insisted.

"June," I said, "There's no way you could know at this stage of the game. All your trust has been shattered and it will take time to find out whether you can trust Walter or not. And Walter, you may have to endure June not trusting you for a very long time."

"I know," he said. He looked down.

The questions continued. She asked about nearly every woman Walter could name. She asked whether drinking was involved. Whether he'd been high on drugs for some of it. Where it happened. How he had met them. How often he had slept with them. Whether he had sought them out or they had sought him. And most painfully, what he loved about the three he'd named as special.

One was a brilliant composer. Another a stunning model. The third a social activist. All claimed to love him.

"What was sex like with each of them?"

"Wait, June," John interrupted. "Are you sure you want to know that? Because what you learn is going to create more images in your head that may never leave you. They may plague you for life. I'd suggest not asking that question."

"You're probably right," she replied. "I just don't understand it. We've been good together for years. In bed, included. It just doesn't make sense. I don't know how to live with this."

John and I nodded.

"It is excruciating," I said. "But I don't think any of us, you included, Walter, really understand how all of this came about. But I think we'll get there in time."

Walter grabbed hold of my last comment.

"I don't understand it either, June. Because you're right. I have been happy with you, and I love you so much. I always have."

June coldly stared at him. "I don't believe you."

It would be a long road for these two.

The next day June spent several more hours asking questions. But as we approached the lunch hour, her questions waned. Walter had answered every one that he could and had listened deeply to her anguish and fury. Only once did he slide into defensiveness, but then quickly caught himself and reversed course, acknowledging the truth in what June was saying. Over and over again he apologized. Often he cried.

After lunch we talked about Walter's earlier years, looking for clues to his promiscuity. Although his behavior suggested a sexual addiction, it didn't quite fit. There wasn't the expected pattern of compulsively searching out partners, using sex to numb pain, needing more and more of it, and feeling agitated and troubled when not getting it. There were months at a time when his work precluded having sexual contact with anyone. He reported those times as fine and not troubling to him.

But as we combed through his earlier years, an interesting detail came to light, or rather, the lack of one. Having been raised Catholic, he noted that he had been an altar boy as a kid. But he couldn't remember the name or the face of the priest he had served despite having shared the altar with him weekly for several years. For that matter, he couldn't remember much about the church either. It all seemed hazy. A back room where the priest robed himself for Mass seemed especially foggy. He kept returning to talk of that room. I asked him if he could picture the door to it. Then the doorknob. It was brass and old. I asked him to imagine reaching for it and opening it. Involuntarily he shuddered.

"What was that, Walter?"

"I don't want to go in," he said.

"It's okay. You don't have to if you don't want to. It's up to you. But I wonder why you're so frightened right now."

"I hate that room," he said.

"Oh," I said.

Gradually the rest spilled out. The priest, his face, his hands, his penis, and where his penis went. It was an ugly story of abuse. Images came flooding back to Walter along with a flashback of rectal penetration and knife-like pain. He had been 11. In those years he wondered whether he was gay, a "faggot," as his family called it, like the ones his dad and brothers openly hated. How could he face his family if it turned out he was? Nightmares had destroyed his sleep for months. Later as an adolescent, he had drunk and drugged his way past them. Eventually his memories faded into fog.

Then at 19, he'd met June. She was his saving grace. Her beauty eclipsed any other girl's. He fell deeply in love and knew he had nothing to fear. He wasn't gay.

But in the background he still wondered, was he gay and just escaping the truth? Or maybe, was he a lover of both sexes? His homophobia was palpable. He still wasn't at peace.

He felt happy with June. But after the kids were born, she rarely seemed happy with him. It seemed like whatever he did wasn't enough. She never seemed to appreciate his contributions. If he helped around the house, she ended up doing his chores over again. If he took the kids to the playground, he stupidly forgot their coats. If he drove them to school, one of them complained to her that he drove too fast. If he made dinner for everyone, he skimped on the vegetables.

He grew more and more angry, more and more defensive. He stopped offering to help. Then he stopped helping altogether. June felt overwhelmed and exhausted. Their fights worsened. Sex tapered down to a trickle.

Then came the day when Walter got a momentous telephone call. After that, his fame catapulted him all over the globe. As his miles traveled grew exponentially, so did his riches. The couple acquired a second home, then a third, plus maids and managers to care for them. They told themselves, "We're in hog heaven."

But every now and then, Walter's sexual self-questioning poked through his exuberance, deflating him like a pin-pricked balloon. The late-night girls were his answer. "I'll show you I'm not a homo," he mumbled to himself. But the dark thoughts didn't abate. Neither did his affairs. After he told the first few lies to June, the rest came easily. He hated himself. But that didn't stop him. He just silenced the thoughts with alcohol. It became a merry-go-round of sex, lies, and scotch. Then on the night June followed him, it all came crashing down. Now Walter was suffering the consequences.

It wouldn't have been hard for John and me to think, "Well, you deserved it, you cheater. Plenty of others have been molested, but most of them don't cheat on their wives." Or, "You're broken, a real mess. You don't deserve this woman and you sure as heck shouldn't be around those kids. What a bad role model." Or, "You call yourself a good Christian? What a joke. You know where you're going in the afterlife, right?" Or a slew of other judgmental thoughts.

During Walter's story, I have to admit, a few of these thoughts did cross my mind. I wondered whether this guy was redeemable. Was he for real or was he pulling the wool over our eyes like he did with June? Did he make up that abuse story to get himself taken off the hook? It was hard to know for sure.

That's where our ninth principle came in handy. We would do no good for this couple if we ascended to the pulpit and pointed our collective finger down at him. We could sheath the word *sinner* in psychobabble, calling him too narcissistic, perhaps, or "manically hypersexual," but what good would that do? We'd be nailing him while ignoring both his history and, more important, the dynamics of the relationship itself. His road with June hadn't been smooth. They'd tripped over how they managed conflict and stumbled into holes carved out by June's criticism and his defensiveness. Instead of attempting to even out rough spots with some healthy discussion, they turned away from their problems and each other. Then along came fame and glory and money that buried their marriage in mud. Now the question was, could they dig out from under it? Certainly not if we didn't examine everything in the marriage, not just Walter's foibles and flaws.

By the end of the first marathon, June agreed to at least keep working on the marriage. She wasn't ready to have Walter live with her and the kids yet. But he could visit weekly. In order for her to believe he was sincere, she told Walter that he had to take a year off from his work, like it or not, to focus on the relationship. He didn't object. It would take a couple of months to set that up, but he'd do it.

So far, the couple had come to understand how Walter's abuse history could have spawned his infidelity and how he used alcohol and drugs to silence his guilt. They were also beginning to see how their conflict management littered with Four Horsemen had torn their connection apart. Finally they had both copped to being blinded by the bright lights of Walter's fame and the havoc it wreaked. They had fallen prey to it and become enslaved by it. Now they wanted their lives back and, if possible, their marriage.

It took three more marathons of hard work. Walter atoned again and again. June rode out the waves of her PTSD, and gradually they grew less intense and frequent. As we settled into Phase Two work, they zeroed in on their conflict issues—work versus family balance and different parenting styles. Resolving each issue wasn't as important as learning new ways to discuss them. They also honed self-soothing methods to keep themselves from flooding, which helped calm down their conflict discussions enormously.

One marathon focused only on the balance of time issue. Walter needed to unearth why his work was so meaningful for him. June explained how much their children missed him and needed a father—at home, not on the road. Then under her breath she whispered how much she also missed him when he was gone.

After seven months and three marathons, Walter moved back home, and they spent his promised year together practicing new ways of talking about everything—conflicts, tasks, daily events, and dreams. In a fourth marathon, they reshaped how their future could be less frenetic and more connected. That was our last time together. Only after the last marathon did June express a desire to resume their sexual life. Together they let us know with a very slyly written postcard.

This couple worked hard. Slowly they rebuilt their love and along with it Marriage # 2. Our love for them grew, too. They were a gift to us. They showed us how even from the dregs, a marriage can be resurrected. But only when we're down in the trenches with a couple and not pointing fingers from on high, a good lesson to remember.

Bringing It Into Practice

- Suspend your own moral judgment when extramarital affairs are revealed.
- Do not keep the affair of one partner a secret from the other. It must be disclosed.

- Do not treat a couple until the affair has ended.
- Support the partner who had the affair as well as the betrayed partner.
- Explain to the couple that the betrayed partner may be suffering from PTSD.
- The betrayed partner needs to express feelings, ask questions and hear words of atonement before working on relationship problems.
- The betraying partner's absolute transparency is necessary in order to repair the relationship.
- Give hope by explaining that Marriage #1 may be gone, but Marriage #2 can be built with a stronger foundation of trust.

10

THE TENTH PRINCIPLE

Dive Deep to Create Shared Meaning

Victor Frankl is a hero of ours. He was a Jewish psychiatrist who lived in Vienna when Hitler rose to power. Choosing to stay beside his parents rather than run, he was carted off to a concentration camp and was the only family member to survive three of them, including Dachau. While imprisoned, he studied his fellow inmates, searching for the secrets to how they survived. It wasn't their skill at scarfing up crumbs. It was their ability to transcend being treated like vermin. While being starved into skeletons, they embodied the pinnacle of what it means to be human. They found meaning in the meaningless, purpose in the impossible. Their spiritual strength transported them past the ovens into liberation. Frankl found himself one of them. After the war he immigrated to the United States where he developed a new therapy out of the shards of his experience. He called it, Logotherapy.

Logotherapy presumes that most psychic pain results from human existential emptiness. When people lack a sense of life purpose, energy drains away, leaving them sad and listless. They don't fully live. Instead, they drift through air like specks of lint. They land here and there but plant themselves nowhere. It is the therapist's job to help them find meaning for their lives that can fill up the emptiness within.

We now know that genetics and unfortunate stresses can tie the mind in knots. But we also believe Frankl had a point. He said people "search for meaning." In the best relationships, a sense of shared meaning and purpose bonds partners together. We saw this in our studies. While partners spent time in our apartment lab, the best masters spent hours discussing their future dreams, what legacies they wished to leave behind, and what values they wanted to role model for their kids. Their conversations traveled fathoms deep. They weren't afraid to acknowledge the reality of their own deaths and their awareness of their limited time. They wanted to make a difference. Regardless of what jobs they did, how many years of education they had, and what talents they embodied, they wanted their lives to mean something. They wanted to contribute something, no matter how small, to their world.

Partners didn't have to embrace identical life goals. They just had to comprehend each other's goals and what made them meaningful. In fact, their values and beliefs could widely diverge. Compatibility of passions and interests wasn't the point. What mattered was talking about them and describing their dreams to one another and finding ways to support each other in realizing them. They understood that to ensure their relationships would last a lifetime, they needed to discuss, understand, and support each other's life purpose.

We added two floors to our Sound Relationship House theory to honor this human need for meaning: the sixth floor, "honor each other's dreams," and the seventh and top floor, "create shared meaning."

In our research we noticed that happy couples inhabited these levels but distressed couples shunned them. In discussing their issues, successful couples willingly dug down to uncover what gave their lives meaning while unhappy partners lingered on the surface.

We knew it wouldn't be enough to calm down conflicts, soothe riddled heart rates, and ratchet up the romance. We had to help partners open up what lay below: their deepest motivations and dreams. We also knew that regardless of education, economic status, or IQ, every person we served was a philosopher, a maker of meaning. Our therapy wouldn't be complete without including an existential focus.

So we come to our tenth principle for doing effective couples therapy: Dive deep to create shared meaning.

The story of one of my favorite couples demonstrates the beauty of deep-diving with clients. I'll call them Jack and Jasmine. They first met at a music festival when Jack was 18 and Jasmine was 16. Jack came from a Samoan heritage. Both his parents were teachers. But at home, the parental bed was bloody with violence and saturated with affairs. In fact, Jack's dad once counseled him: "You should always have one main woman with lots of others on the side." Dad also chiseled away any confidence Jack built with constant criticism and contempt. At the age of 12, Jack entered the drug-dealing world. Fueled with anger, he hustled his way up the ladder. By 18, he had a dozen underlings working for him. By 26, he was pulling in $20,000 a week .

Jasmine was raised in the projects. Her parents were African American; both were victims of ghetto life. Dad landed in jail for drug-related charges and Mom was a hard-living addict. At the age of two, Jasmine was handed off to her grandmother to raise. Not a cookies-and-milk coddler, this grandma fed Jasmine on slaps and criticism. At age eight, Jasmine was moved to her aunt and uncle's place. They already had lots of kids and stayed high most of the time. Uncle soon began to "fiddle" with Jasmine and later invited his friends to share in the fun. She was incested and abused from age 8 to age 13. It finally stopped when Uncle moved down to target the next in line, Jasmine's younger cousins.

When Jasmine met Jack at the festival, he matched her dream to a T. Tall and dark, she spotted him as he gleefully rocked a baby, a little cousin of his. She loved the way his long eyelashes curled up and his pencil-thin beard outlined his jaw. She dreamed his big broad hands could protect her. Jack noticed her gaze and strolled over to her. He liked her outfit and what filled it. But she was with another boy and hurried away. Months later they happened to meet at a bus stop. This time they were alone. Jack managed to get her number before they parted.

They talked for hours by phone and then dated. At ages 17 and 19, they moved in together. To bind him to her, Jasmine waited on him hand and foot. A year later, they had their first child. Over the next five years, they added three more. Money poured in, but so did guns and the number of their friends who died. Jack's fortunes rose in the drug world, but so did his paranoia. Soon their guns outweighed their kids. When a girlfriend asked Jasmine about her future plans, she flatly said, "Well, I'll either be in prison, a prison wife, or dead. Those are the only options."

A few years passed. One morning Jasmine woke up with a horrible feeling. Something wasn't right. Jack had already taken off for the day in his new souped-up truck. Two hours later she got a call. It was Jack's cousin.

"Did you hear?" he asked. He sounded frantic.

"Hear what?"

She overheard him whisper to somebody in the background, "Should I tell her?"

"Yeah, man. Tell her!"

"Jack's been shot. They've taken him to the hospital."

When she arrived there, they told her the guy with the tattoo had died.

"What did the tattoo look like?" she asked.

Thank God it wasn't his.

Jack was in surgery for 12 hours to remove five bullets from his chest. Some guy had tried to hijack his truck and shot him at close range. Twice he died on the table but was revived. After he came to in recovery, he mumbled to Jasmine, "I saw Christ."

She was dumbfounded. A week later he said, "We're going to leave this life."

A year later, they had. It took determination and drive. No more big bucks. They crowded into a cheap apartment and worked on becoming lay pastors. They wanted to minister to kids destined for ghetto life like they had once been. In another year Jack was promoted to direct a special program for teens with Jasmine working under him. Their collegial relationship grew tense. Jack's perfectionism and tough supervision made a mess of Jasmine's confidence. She grew downcast at work and silent at home. Soon she fled whatever rooms Jack stepped into. He began to insert his massive body between her and the exit.

It was around this time that I met them. John and I were filming interviews I conducted with hard-scrabble couples trying to survive poverty. (The interviews served as material for a new program funded by the Federal Administration of Children and Families to help poor couples' stay together as they transitioned to parenthood.) Jack and Jasmine were one of these couples. They stood out as bright, articulate, and unafraid to share their story. We felt a deep connection immediately.

A few months later, they phoned me. They wanted therapy. They were having too many fights and growing more distant by the day. I agreed to see them at a tenth of my usual fee. Our early work focused on better conflict management. They especially needed to work on flooding; they tried different self-soothing methods until they each found one that fit them well.

Midway through our sessions together, they came in looking forlorn. Jack appeared particularly upset. Once I heard their update, it was no wonder. A terrible event had occurred in their community. Jack was terribly stressed by it and needed to talk. It seemed a good time to teach them how to do a "Stress-Reducing Conversation," an exercise John and I invented that teaches partners how to support each other when one is stressed by a situation outside the relationship.

The need for this exercise originated from some research conducted by John's colleague at the University of Washington, Neil Jacobson. Jacobson had created his own form of couples therapy that was based on partners accepting one another without trying to change each other. When he analyzed the results of his method, he found an important difference between the couples whose improvements lasted and the couples who relapsed. The couples who maintained their changes found ways to discuss their life stresses, while those who relapsed failed to give each other support during stressful times. The stresses emanated from outside the relationship, like those a partner experienced on the job or in a relationship with a friend. The ability to manage external stresses together was the key to preventing relapse for these couples.

When we looked at our own lab couples, we noticed that relationship masters also supported each other in managing external stress. Their conversations gave a wide berth to problem solving and centered on empathetic listening instead. Listeners didn't offer advice until asked to do so. They questioned their partner to understand what made the stress so bad and offered compassionate statements of empathy. Sometimes listeners commiserated with their partners by sharing their own similar stories, but we noticed they never took over the conversation by diverting all the focus onto themselves. They would briefly mention a similar experience but then quickly return to their partner's story. They would also never side with the "enemy," the person their partner was complaining about, by trying to justify that person's behavior, for example. They would simply take their partner's side and at the least, join in the emotions their partner was expressing. In short, they worked hard to be their partner's ally. They seemed to understand that what would help their partner the most was to feel less alone with their stress, not just hear a quick fix for the problem.

John and I fashioned an exercise based on what we saw our successful couples do to manage their external stress. One partner would be the listener while the other partner described his or her stress. The stress had to originate from outside the relationship and be separate from it, the kind of story that a question like, "How was your day?" might elicit. The listener's job was to ask questions first that showed interest and concern. Some examples might include, "What was the most upsetting part about this for you?" or "What are you most worried about here?" or simply, "Tell me more." The listener also needed to express empathy for the speaker's feelings with statements like, "What a bummer," "That sounds terrible," or "No wonder you feel worried. I would, too." The listener might share personal stories that related to the one the speaker was describing, but only briefly, after which the speaker could once again claim the floor. The toughest job for the listener would be to avoid problem solving, unless the speaker specifically requested help with it.

I introduced this exercise to Jasmine and Jack when Jack opened up our session with the following story:

During the week a local gang member had gunned down another young man from an enemy gang. A spate of violence had followed. Jack had been called in to cool down tempers. But two higher-level pastors had crowded him out, despite their having had no experience with gang warfare, a world Jack knew well. Jack was sidelined and left feeling impotent.

I told Jack to describe his feelings to Jasmine. She would serve as listener, asking questions and providing empathy without trying to problem solve.

Jack said, "I'm pissed off. They had no right to butt in. I think they were just doing it so they could claim all the credit. Especially when the reporters stopped by. They're idiots! They have no idea what they're doing."

Jasmine replied, "No wonder you're mad. They're not gonna stop this killing. It's just gonna go on. That must be awful for you."

"Yeah. And there's nothing I can do about it. This one pastor—he's done nothing to reach out. I've been the one to reach out to those kids. They know me. Then comes an opportunity for the spotlight? Here he comes, taking over. He pushes me to the side. What am I supposed to do? I don't know. . . . Maybe I'm just looking to be the hero. But I want to stop the killing. I could do it better . . . At least I think I could."

I bent over and whispered to Jasmine, "Try asking him what's the worst part about this situation for him."

She asked, "What's upsetting you the most, baby?"

Jack raised his hand and covered his eyes.

He mumbled, "That I'm a failure."

I said to Jasmine, "Ask him, even though it seems obvious, what would be so upsetting about that."

"Baby, if you were a failure, what would be the worst thing about that?"

". . . That what my Dad said was right." His face crumpled. Here was this big tough guy with eyes wet, a sure sign to dig deeper.

Jasmine immediately reached for his hand. "Jack, I love your father, but he was the most wrong man on the planet. He hated himself so much that he tried to kill what was inside of you. Everything you do is brilliant. Everything you touch turns to gold. No one can hold a candle to you."

"That was wonderfully insightful, Jasmine, and so loving," I said. This seemed a good time to bring in the tenth principle. I said to her, "Try to ask him something about succeeding here. Why is it so important to him?"

"Okay. What kind of success do you want here, Jack? And why is it so important to you?"

There was a long pause. "I saw so many senseless killings. Christ, I was almost one of them. And these kids are so young, younger even than I was. Their lives are all about killing each other off, just like mine was. I can't stand it. It's such a waste. I got lucky. But that last kid, the one who was 19, he wasn't lucky. He's gone for good. If I can't do something to rescue these kids, to get 'em off the streets and into better lives, what's the point of my living, especially after that truck hijacking? I was given a new life. I was resurrected. It's got to mean something. That's why I've got to get in there and show them how wrong this is, that there's a better way, that they can make it out just like I did." Jack looked hard at her.

Jasmine hugged him. She breathed into his ear, "Yeah."

They spent their remaining time that day outlining how to actualize Jack's vision.

Although politics prevailed this time around, by unearthing Jack's deeper feelings and search for meaning, they had begun to weld together a new life purpose that could forge them into an unstoppable team.

One day towards the end of our work together, Jasmine came in with bright eyes and a new issue. She asked Jack to please buy her little gifts to show he loved her. She appreciated the big presents he gave her at Christmas and on her birthday. But there were long stretches of time in which she received nothing. She laughed, saying, "Maybe it's all those late-night infomercials I watch. But I'm ready for diamonds. I'm ready for tennis bracelets. . . "

Jack spit out, "I'm ready for debt. I'm ready for bankruptcy . . ."

Jasmine looked crushed.

"Wait a moment," I said. It looks like you have very different positions on gift giving. Is that right?"

"We always have," said Jasmine.

"So why don't we do a Dream-Within-Conflict discussion here?" I suggested.

The Dream-Within-Conflict exercise is one of my favorites. It also originated from John's master couples who excelled at conflict management; it especially helps couples dive deep into their own and each other's dreams, values, and visions. In studying the masters' videotapes we saw that when they were gridlocked on an important conflict issue, they switched gears, shifted into first and slowed everything down. One partner became the speaker while the other listened. Listeners avoided bringing up an opposing position or arguing against their partner's position. They only asked the speaker questions to more fully understand their partner's position. Their questions invited the speaker to dive deep and open up the subterranean world where old traumas lurked, dreams lay hidden, and a sense of legacy and purpose nourished their inner life.

In reflecting on this exercise, I remembered one important night early in my own marriage when John and I were gridlocked with a relationship dilemma. I desperately wanted to own a little cabin out in the wilds, but John thought it was a ridiculous idea. Being the son of Holocaust survivors and a child refugee himself, he reminded me that one could never be sure, we might have to make a quick escape like his parents had.

"All they took with them was a lemon, a package of sugar, and the clothes on their back. Accumulating anything more than what we already have is unnecessary and a waste," he said.

I angrily retorted, "What about all those books you keep buying?"

At some point, we had entered couples therapy to get some help with resolving this issue. (This was long before we had created our own therapy together.)

The therapist loved John, but me, not so much. One day she turned to him and said, "You know, you can just say 'No.' You don't have to respond to her needs, nor do you have to explain yourself."

John turned to me and said, "Do I sound like that?"

I nodded.

We left. That was our last session with her.

Later that night, we pulled out our memories of what those master couples had done with their gridlocked conflict. Haltingly at first, we began to ask each other questions, ones like, "Is there some childhood history or story behind your position on this issue?" and "Is there a deeper goal or purpose in this for you?"

I ended up confiding in John about my childhood days in which I would quietly steal out of the house after everyone had gone to bed, run to the miraculous forest two blocks away, and curl up beneath my favorite tree to sleep. Before sunrise I'd awaken and sneak back upstairs. No one was the wiser. I'd done this once or twice a week for years. The forest was my refuge.

John shared more about his parents, their journey from Vienna over the mountains to Switzerland and to the Dominican Republic, where he was born. It wasn't until the United States finally opened its doors to European Jews in 1945 that he and his family finally made it to New York with almost nothing in their pockets.

After hours of talk, we understood each other so much better. Long story short, a year later I finally got my cabin. And the good news? John fell in love with it, too.

Back in my session with Jack and Jasmine, I shared with them the rudimentary outlines of this story as I reviewed with them how to do a Dream-Within-Conflict exercise. One person would be the speaker (in the exercise, the Dream Speaker) while the other was the listener (the Dream Catcher). Then they would switch roles. I handed each of them a page that listed a number of questions and a set of values. The job of the speaker would be to answer each question the listener asked with as much detailed explanation as possible. Each speaker might want to refer to the list of values on the page (Sample Dreams for the Dream Speaker) when it came time to answer questions about their underlying values and dreams regarding their position on the issue. The job of the listener would be to simply read each question from the list (Sample Questions for the Dream Catcher) to the speaker, one at a time, and listen to the speaker's answers. The listener should take care not to raise their own position on the issue until it was their turn to speak. From time to time I might pop in to fine-tune a question if I thought we were missing an essential point the speaker needed to mention. Here's a copy of the page I gave them:

SAMPLE QUESTIONS FOR THE DREAM CATCHER (THE LISTENER)

1. Do you have any core beliefs, ethics, or values that are part of your position on this issue?
2. Is there a story behind this for you, or does this relate to your background or childhood history in some way?
3. Tell me why this is so important to you.
4. What feelings do you have about this issue?
5. What would be your ideal dream here?
6. Is there a deeper purpose or goal in this for you?
7. What do you wish for?
8. What do you need?
9. Is there a fear or disaster scenario in not having this dream honored?

SAMPLE DREAMS FOR THE DREAM SPEAKER

1. A sense of freedom
2. The experience of peace
3. Unity with nature
4. Exploring who I am
5. Adventure
6. A spiritual journey
7. Justice
8. Honor
9. Unity with my past
10. Healing
11. Knowing my family
12. Becoming all I can be
13. Having a sense of power
14. Dealing with my aging
15. Exploring a creative side of myself
16. Becoming more powerful
17. Getting over past hurts

18. Becoming more competent
19. Asking God for forgiveness
20. Exploring an old part of myself I have lost
21. Getting over a personal hang-up
22. Having a sense of order
23. Being able to be productive
24. A place and a time to just "be"
25. Being able to truly relax
26. Reflecting on my life
27. Getting my priorities in order
28. Finishing something important
29. Exploring the physical side of myself
30. Being able to compete and win
31. Travel
32. Quietness
33. Atonement
34. Building something important
35. Ending a chapter of my life
36. Saying goodbye to something
37. Love

Jasmine opted to be the first speaker. In response to the first question, she replied, "I think gifts are a tangible sign that you love me. Every time I look at the gift, I remember your love. I have a hard time remembering it sometimes. It's love that I can see and touch."

"Is there some childhood history that is part of your position here?" Jack asked.

She got quiet. With one finger she tapped the couch. "I never got any gifts. At Christmas my aunt's kids got so many presents they would stretch from under the tree all the way to the door. Somebody would say, 'What about Jasmine?' Then they'd go grab a pack of socks and give that to me. They wouldn't even wrap it. I thought if I just gave a lot to everyone, they'd give me something back someday. But it didn't happen . . ." She looked very sad.

She went on to speak of loss, emptiness, abandonment, and profound pain—the colors of her childhood. Jack giving her something especially when he wasn't obligated to do so meant the world to her. She was finally visible, someone who deserved to be cherished. Even the smallest gift would mean she had left that ugly cold world behind and could now open to the wonder of being loved. Jack had no idea how significant gifts were to Jasmine before now and how her childhood had shaped their meaning for her. Once he heard her replies, he visibly softened.

Jack's answers weren't so different from Jasmine's, at first. He said he never received gifts either when he was young. Not until his godmother came along. She was incredible. She showered him with every toy, every game he'd ever wanted.

But at the same time Jack's dad had pounded into him an

important lesson. Trust no one. You can bring them in close, he'd said, but don't ever trust them. Jack pointed out that his dad had been right, because even his godmother had left.

"Oh, I understood why," he said. "That was during my teenage years, when I was getting into the game. Things got dangerous back then. I don't blame her for leaving. But then my hurt turned to anger. I didn't trust anybody then. If anybody gave me anything, I'd think, 'What are they trying to get from me?' I'd just look at them with . . ." He searched for the word.

"Suspicion?" I asked.

"Yeah." He paused.

"Jack, as long as you suspect why someone is giving you a gift, you won't be able to take in the love that might be accompanying that gift. The suspicion will block it out."

"Yeah, I suppose."

"Do you think that might be happening when Jasmine gives you a gift?"

"Maybe."

They returned to their discussion. Jack wanted to please Jasmine but feared that their limited bank account wouldn't suffice to make her happy. She shook her head and said it didn't matter what the gift was, because as the old saying went, "It's the thought that counts," and for her, doubly so. He grasped that Jasmine didn't need diamonds or tennis bracelets but just a little something that showed he was thinking of her, not because he had to but because he loved her, pure and simple. Such gestures would mean the world to her. Jasmine also wanted him to work on receiving gifts more graciously from her. After Jack delved into more questions he realized that the little things he received from Jasmine would mean he was a different man than the son his father had raised—someone who valued love above only looking out for himself and who had the courage to take in love and to be trusting rather than closed off and alone. In turn, he could pass down this important lesson to his children by role modeling it rather than the distrust his father had taught him.

Over the following months, Jack and Jasmine's relationship grew even stronger. He would surprise her now and then with a small treat, and the gesture made her ecstatic, she said. Jack bowed in thanks when Jasmine bestowed a gift on him.

One day they came in and reported great news. Together they had won a grant to open up a teen center in the projects where Jasmine had once lived. Soon after hearing this, they had their final session.

From time to time Jasmine has emailed me about how they are doing. Their teen center has expanded to include six programs. At the time of this writing, she has also begun taking psychology classes at a community college in hopes of advancing to a four-year university. From there she hopes to pursue graduate work. Jack is now running a larger umbrella organization under which the teen center operates.

Both are fulfilling their shared life purpose. There was no doubt that they would.

Bringing It Into Practice

- Every person is a philosopher.
- Shared meaning can unite a couple.

- You may have to dig deep to help a couple find their shared meaning.
- Gridlocked conflicts often contain underlying values and dreams. Help couples to talk about them.
- Relationships grow stronger when partners support each other's life dreams.

11

Hold the Hope

All of us face new couples with a question: Can they make it? Sometimes they look so bad we add: *Should* they make it? We have warning signs that couples therapy is contraindicated. Severe domestic violence is one. When we face a couple with characterological domestic violence, the best we can do is tell them couples therapy is premature for now, then refer each of them for individual therapy and work hard to help the victim seek a safe retreat.

There are additional contraindications for couples work. If one partner is flagrantly psychotic, he or she should be guided to seek individual psychiatric care, with an additional referral for the healthier partner if desired. If one partner is actively suicidal, the same recommendation applies. Couples therapy is too tough an arena for people this fragile. Once they are stabilized and out of danger, couples therapy can be considered.

How about couples who look hopeless but don't pose a risk of danger? These are ones we may diagnose as personality disordered, mood disordered, substance-addicted, or so traumatized it makes our eyes crossed. The ground of our work begins here. This is the starting and ending point; it underlies every one of our principles and is the foundation for them: Hold the hope.

John and I often see couples with assessment scores that could sink a battleship. A couple may crawl up to our door with scores of 8 and 11 on the Locke-Wallace scale that measures marital satisfaction, whereas average couples score around 100 and happy couples 115 or higher. We've seen partners where one is so riddled by Borderline Personality features that the office splits in two, good and bad, as she heads through the door, while her husband's grandiosity elevates him to the ceiling. We've seen couples where a man has one foot in our office but the other in Tahiti because his partner drinks a fifth of vodka every night. The good news is that these couples are flesh and blood, not stone—they have the capacity for change. Evolution has gifted them with a marvelous drive towards adaptation and survival, although sometimes adaptability has hindered them. They may have already twisted themselves into pretzels trying to become their partner's ideal. As a case in point, we saw one couple where the wife had clearly been gorgeous from the very beginning. Yet by the age of 35, she had undergone breast and gluteal implants, downsized her waistline through lower rib removal, and had a face-lift, all to please her man. On the other hand, he had a belly the size of Ohio. This husband told his wife she still didn't look feminine enough. In a moment of exasperation, John wryly noted, "You know, you're no Adonis."

Can these relationships change? Yes.

The toughest challenge for us is to spot the glimmer of hope that hibernates deep inside a relationship. The couple won't see it at first. In fact, they'll moan with hopelessness. Their despair may weigh so much that after they leave, you'll want to jump off a bridge or leap into a new career. In my college days I worked as a hotel maid cleaning up the messes of guests with the aid of various chemicals. On my bad days as a therapist, I wonder if I am I still doing that job.

Our saving grace is knowing that change is possible. Even in the worst relationships, fire-breathing couples can walk in with singed hair and walk out holding hands a year later. It's miraculous.

We also know that some won't make it. In my 30 years of couples work, I've only told one couple to call it quits in a case where the usual contraindications didn't exist. This was a couple John and I saw together.

Heather had been married to Gary for six years. She had suffered incest in childhood and rape at 21, with no treatment for either. Needless to say, she had some qualms about sex. She met Gary at a gym. He was a professional body builder, or so he said. In reality he snorted cocaine and preyed on women like a flea on a juicy dog. Heather wanted him to go to rehab and then find work. She had supported them both since the time they married. He insisted the job market was tough enough without rehab messing up his records.

It was clear to us that Gary was ruled by addiction and his need to deceive. We could have tried to help him see the self-destructiveness in his addiction: how it blocked him from the stability necessary to nail down a job, how it masked him from his wife as well as from himself, how it was causing his brain to lesion and his brain cells to die, how it was shortening his life, and how treatment could give him a new and better life. We could have helped Heather articulate her pain at living with a third and preferred party in her marriage, cocaine. We could have combed through their relationship, trawling for cracks we could repair. In other cases, we had done work like this that had ended on a positive note.

This case was different. Gary had only one goal in mind. He wanted more sex. Nothing else would do. He didn't care that his addiction was a problem. He didn't care that Heather paid all the bills. He didn't care that they weren't close and had bad quarrels. He didn't care that she hurt. He particularly didn't care that he was selling off Heather's jewelry and silver and their TV and stereo to fund his cocaine habit and that this upset her. In our opinion, the worst was this: He didn't care that sex was difficult for her if not impossible, given her history of rape and abuse. He was sick of hearing about it. He'd heard about it once already and that was enough. Get on with it. If we couldn't make her more sexual, why should they keep coming to us?

We'll admit it: We really didn't like this guy. He seemed pretty heartless. Maybe there was some tenderness tucked way down in there, beneath the mounds of white powder he snorted every day. But we sure couldn't find it. For several sessions, we looked hard. We used every technique up our sleeve: The Dan Wile intervention to dramatize Heather's terror in the bedroom; the Dream-Within-Conflict exercise to talk about the meaning of sex; the Rituals of Connection exercise to bridge the canyon between them. Nothing worked. Nothing changed, at least in Gary's head. He wanted sex. That was it. And Heather was too afraid to give it to him. Yes, she could split off from herself and perform, but she would end up lying on her back like a zombie while some part of her numbly looked on from the ceiling. In short she could reenact being an abuse victim—not exactly love-making.

Through a number of sessions Heather cried while Gary looked on, impassive and cold. Finally there was one where we faced our own hopelessness. There was no getting through his walls. Either we just weren't good enough therapists, or this marriage was impossible to change. After this session, we decided to call it quits. The next time, I met with Heather alone. I told her we were out of options. As far as we could tell, the chances of change were nil. With words I'd never spoken before, I forecast that this marriage was doomed. If Heather chose to stay married, there was a good chance she would lose everything financially, going into massive debt and perhaps even bankruptcy. It was also likely that Gary would have multiple affairs, if he wasn't doing so already. Some suspicious behavior of his had already set off our alarm bells. We doubted he would ever stop demanding that she become his sex kitten. Instead he'd deny her time to heal from her sexual abuse. In fact, he'd likely open up new wounds. She could stay in the marriage, but it would likely kill off her soul or at least drive it underground. Was it worth it?

She decided no, it wasn't and left him. We were deeply relieved. As far as we could tell, this was a relationship that needed to end. Hope itself was contraindicated. She decided to pursue treatment for herself instead.

Abe and Laurie were the opposite of Heather and Gary. They, too, had a marriage badly scarred by Laurie's childhood sexual abuse. Laurie was raised on a farm in upstate New York. She was the only child of a dad who drank himself to sleep every night and a mom who perpetually stayed wrapped in her bathrobe. Laurie's grandfather lived with them, too, upstairs above the hay in the barn. Laurie was a tomboy who reveled in climbing trees and padding through the woods. When she got lonely, she talked to the birds perched high overhead.

Laurie first came to me alone. Her sexuality was broken, and she didn't know why. Before she married Abe, they had made love daily. Their sex life was tender and passionate. But on their honeymoon night after making love, a strange despair gripped her, driving her to curl up on the floor like a snail under its shell. From then on, their sex life slid down a cliff into oblivion. It had been seven years since they had made love. Furthermore, she'd banned Abe from undressing in front of her and sleeping in anything less than work clothes. They still slept in the same room. But fully clothed, Laurie parked herself in a sleeping bag on the floor while Abe stayed in the bed.

Downstairs Laurie stepped out of rooms the minute Abe entered them. She was like a scared rabbit running from a gun-toting hunter. He'd turn left; she'd cut right. Even in their rose garden, if he moved closer than 20 yards from her, she'd back up a row or two to increase the distance. Despair filled their home like carbon monoxide, slowly suffocating them.

All of this bewildered Laurie and broke her heart and surely her partner's, too. She was desperate. Why was this happening to her? Was she going crazy? Why did it begin as soon as they stepped across the marriage threshold, especially when they had been so happy before?

Once we settled into our individual work together, Laurie brought in a series of dreams. Each one featured dark stairs leading upward. With each progressive dream, Laurie ventured up more steps. The higher she climbed, the darker it got, and the more frightened she became. Finally in one dream she reached for a doorknob at the top, but awakened sweating in panic before she could open the door. I wondered if these were the steps that led up to her grandfather's room. One day we were talking about him. I asked her if she had visited his room before. When she said yes, I asked her if she could draw a picture of it. She detailed every stick of furniture but his bed. I asked her where did he sleep?

She fell silent. Her eyes grew glassy. Her face froze. She sat as still as a mouse facing a rattlesnake's fangs. Not a muscle moved.

"What's happening, Laurie?" I asked, trying not to sound alarmed.

There was no answer.

"Is he there?" I quietly asked.

There was the smallest head nod.

"You're not alone this time," I said. "We're here together now."

She blinked. No words came from her. She sat, and I sat. The silence lasted 25 minutes.

Finally she said, "It's him."

"Your grandfather?"

"Yes."

"Where are you?"

"On the bed."

"Where is he?"

"Above me."

Then she added, "I'm chained down. It hurts."

"Do you want to leave that room, Laurie? Because you can."

"How?"

"This is a memory. You don't have to stay in it if you don't want to. You have the power to come back to this office, to our being together here, without him anywhere near you." I offered her my hand. Her gaze broke, and she looked down. Then she took my hand. Slowly she returned to now. We both took a deep breath.

The next week Laurie told me about a compulsive ritual she had engaged in for years. It was secret; she'd never told anyone about it. When the house was empty, she would dig out a bag of iron clips, chains, and barbells from the back of her closet. She would open the bag, then descend into a trance state, undress and clip the chains onto her nipples and genitals and weigh them down with barbells. She'd face a mirror, masturbate, and have an orgasm. Afterward she'd detach the implements, put away her tools of self-torture, and wake up as if from a dream. For hours afterward she'd writhe in shame, then eventually sleep it off.

In the following sessions Laurie told me what she knew about her grandfather. In 1950 he had immigrated from Germany and come to live with them. Judging by age and the year when he died, he must have been living in Germany and 25–30 years old during World War II. I asked Laurie if she knew anything about his wartime activities. She replied that the family had never talked about it, but she would call them and ask.

After several difficult phone calls, her father finally broke down and admitted that Grandpa had been a Gestapo commandant. His wartime job was to extract information from prisoners at a labor camp, no doubt through torture. When the war ended, the U.S. government had welcomed him with open arms because he supplied them with information about various communists who lived across Europe. Laurie's family hadn't known any of this until Mom, while dusting his desk, had dropped a book on the floor. Out from its pages tumbled some old documents. She read them all. They revealed his terrible history. She never returned to his room again.

Laurie had always had fragments of memories. She had never known their origins. They seemed like scenes from a TV horror show. Now she realized they were *her* horror show. We began to make sense of her behavior with Abe. As long as she remained single, she could be freely sexual with anyone, including Abe. But the minute she married him, he took on the mantle of "family," and to her shadowy unconscious mind, family included old family as well as new. Laurie couldn't distinguish between the two. So Abe was now another potential abuser. Moreover, the height difference between them was no help. He was 6'5", she was 5'1". Their standing face to face, or rather face to chest, triggered Laurie's childhood terror of her grandfather towering over her, preparing for his sadistic sexual acts with her. No wonder she cowered and fled when Abe entered the room.

Laurie's recovery work took two years. With every month that passed, she grew stronger, clearer, more alive and more lighthearted. Best of all, the compulsive ritual that had shadowed her for decades disappeared and never returned.

One day she began our session by announcing, "I want to have a normal sex life. I hate that we can't make love. I can't be a whole person until I get that back. It's been nine years now! My poor husband. It's not fair to him, and it's not fair to me. I want that to change."

"Okay," I said. "That will mean some couples therapy. Would you like me to refer you and Abe to a good couples therapist?"

"No way," she said. "You've seen us. I don't want to start over again."

Laurie and I had traveled a long way together, navigating some terribly difficult waters in the process. The journey itself was bonding. Fearful yet courageous, it was Laurie's relentless drive and her intense desire to heal that had carried us through those nightmarish rapids. I was mostly along for the ride, carrying the faith that she'd eventually make it into calmer waters. Plunging ahead, she had. Now she sought a different shore, one she could share with her husband.

But my doing Laurie's individual *and* couples work? I'd been taught years ago that was a no-no. The internal voices of old supervisors admonished me accordingly. I told them to pipe down, then told Laurie we should think carefully about this. It would mean sharing the attention I'd given her with Abe now. We could still continue our individual sessions, but in the couples work she and I would need to watch for any signs that she felt slighted, overlooked, or invisible, and we'd have to be sure to address them. I'd also have to be careful that Abe didn't feel I was biased in favor of Laurie. It would need to be a careful balancing act. She agreed and still wanted to proceed.

The next week Abe accompanied Laurie to our first couples session. He was tall, thin, and sad-eyed. He had broad shoulders, but they curled in as if someone had just scolded him. After three sessions of assessment I focused mostly on getting to know him. Laurie tolerated this shift of attention well.

Abe grew up with a domineering mother and a doormat of a father. The family revolved around Mom's moods and demands. She was like a black hole that sucked up everyone's attention. Abe had no idea what his own needs were, then or now. Sex was high on the list, but the rest of it was blank. I mentioned that this was unusual. Most people needed more than sex alone. Abe said he had shut down his needs so early he hardly knew what a need was. For half a dozen sessions he grieved his lost self, the part of him that had subsisted on crumbs. For years, he'd received little more, including in this marriage. But he still adored Laurie. He had watched with amazement as she returned to a semblance of the woman he courted years ago.

In tiny increments, we began to work on trust and connection. Laurie needed constant reassurance that Abe wouldn't force sex upon her if she allowed him near her. From sitting on opposite ends of the couch in my office, they inched towards sitting inside the same four walls at home. This took Laurie's learning to self-soothe when DPA took hold and telling Abe when she was anxious so he could quietly give her the space she needed. Gradually they moved on to conflict issues they had skirted, and shored up their skills to resolve them. Next they established a ritual of watching TV together, and then eating their meals together.

For eight months they worked on creating and solidifying their rituals of connection. Then in a pivotal session Laurie announced the day had come; it was time to work on sex. She was still sleeping on the floor in her sleeping bag with Abe in the bed, and he was still relegated to changing clothes in the closet. Would Laurie's demons destroy what they had accomplished to this point? I worried.

Here was the time to grab hold of hope and hang on tight. This woman had suffered the worst sexual abuse I'd heard of in 35 years of work. Her grandfather had taken the same sadistic pleasure in torturing and raping her that he'd enjoyed with his wartime prisoners. The man had to have been a psychopath. He'd devoured Laurie's innocent sexuality as easily as downing a sweet cake. Could Laurie ever get her sexuality back, especially when the familial nature of marriage triggered every piercing memory she had?

Laurie wanted to resurrect her erotic self but deeply feared she couldn't. For Abe, day by day, a sexless life felt more and more impossible. Again, Laurie's despair reared its ugly head, and so did Abe's. For now I needed to stuff down my worries and hold the hope for them.

I asked Laurie to draw a ladder and list a different physical interaction with Abe beside each rung. The rungs would be ranked by how much anxiety they triggered, from lowest to highest. Laurie had to practice her deep breathing to even list the interactions, let alone act them out. Then we broke them down further, making them as incrementally small as possible. Together the three of us became very inventive. Hugs sat on the lowest rung. To remedy the fears she felt when they stood and hugged each other, we started with Abe seated and Laurie standing so she'd be taller. Then she figured out that approaching Abe from behind would feel even safer. That was where we started.

They hugged daily with Laurie sidling around Abe's chair step by step, week by week, until finally they could hug facing each other. Next, Laurie focused on their TV watching ritual. They had been formerly sitting on separate chairs a few yards apart. Now they moved to a couch. It was nine feet long, perfect for progressing from opposite ends to sitting side by side. But as Laurie got within three feet of Abe, she panicked. Their height difference and all it triggered kicked up again. Abe exclaimed that a few phone books would do it! Sure enough, when Laurie perched on these, her panic vanished. Shoulder to shoulder, they gleefully munched popcorn and watched old *I Love Lucy* reruns, eventually holding hands.

Their progress continued. Laurie hit occasional points of panic when they needed to either drop down a rung or linger for longer where they'd landed. That was fine. There was no hurry.

After many months, we finally arrived at their bedroom door. Now the really hard work began. Every tiny step became a reason to celebrate. At this point, I was reminded of something deeply personal that had happened to me. When I had just turned 11, the Sabin polio vaccine was approved and released. All school kids were taking it, nation-wide. Although I had a strangely swollen cheek the night before, my folks said, No worries, go to school and get the vaccine. I did, and became one of four kids in the country to contract polio from it. It turns out, my swollen cheek was mumps, not the insect bite they had surmised. And mumps is a crazy virus. It activated the vaccine that, in turn, gave me polio. It took six months to figure all this out. My leg was paralyzed. There was daily shock therapy for a year and a half. Though nobody talked about it, I think we had just about lost hope by then, and I resigned myself to living with a brace for life. But then, a miracle happened. My big toe twitched—maybe just a millimeter or two. But it moved. Then the next week, three millimeters. Month by month, my progress crept forwards. Finally the day came to try to walk between parallel bars but with no leg brace.

That particular triumphant morning came back to me as Laurie confronted her bedroom terror. By then, she had drawn a second ladder. This one detailed every inch of change from sleeping bag to bed to bath and back to bed again and then on to touch, all the way from the non-erotic to intercourse.

It had been over a year of therapy at this point. Step by step, we'd learned a lot. Laurie always needed her head to be at least level with Abe's. When they cuddled (at that point, fully clothed and on top of the covers) she could hold him with his head on her shoulder, but never vice versa. They took a huge leap forwards when they began to bathe together, first under cover of bubbles, and then without them. Laurie needed to frequently ground herself by looking into Abe's eyes and hearing his voice, a far galaxy from her grandfather's.

You can probably guess how the story ends. It was like the mythical tale of Andromeda and Perseus. Andromeda had been chained to a rock to sate the appetite of a devouring sea monster. With great bravery, Perseus faced down the beast and rescued her. In our story, Laurie released herself from her chains, and hand in hand she and her prince defeated the monster together. Their intimacy was reborn, now more rich with meaning and passion than ever.

That day on the parallel bars, I took my first two steps. Then the next week, a few more. Slowly, nerves woke up and muscles strengthened. I've been climbing peaks ever since.

So have Abe and Laurie. For a while, I held the hope for them. Then they took over and harbored it themselves.

For every couple we see, we can begin with hope. Time, plus some good hard work, will tell whether our hope is warranted. We hope you take it on. For a couples therapist, there's almost nothing more satisfying than watching a relationship rise from the ashes, strong and loving.

Bringing It Into Practice

- Hold the hope for clients if they can't feel it themselves.

Conclusion

As we look around today, our world is full of battles large and small. Countries tear themselves apart. Alliances form one year and fall apart the next. Meaningless bloodshed reddens the land. Refugees run from one border to the next, seeking safe harbor. What can we do?

If you're like us, it can feel pretty overwhelming. As a couples therapist, you have a chance to create change. Whether between nations or partners, respect has been lost and compassion has gone missing. It doesn't have to remain so. People in relationships can change. Sometimes all they need is knowing the alternatives to old destructive practices. Sometimes they need more—reformation, rehabilitation, even somehow resurrection. Fundamentally, at every point, they face a choice. Do we choose to love here or to hate? To pull away or approach and touch?

As couples therapists, all we can do is lay out their choices, then watch from the sidelines. If they make the choice to love, it's an affirmation of what's best in humanity, the ability to understand, feel compassion, and love again. What a privilege it is to see this! At those times we can know that in some small way we've helped bring a little more love into the world. We hope you join us by helping the couples who come to your door.

References

Bach, G. R., & Wyden, P. (1983). *The intimate enemy: How to fight fair in love and marriage*. New York: Avon.

Doherty, W. (1999). *The intentional family*. New York: William Morrow.

Frankl, V. (2006). *Man's search for meaning*. Boston, MA: Beacon Press

Glass, S., & Staeheli, J. C. (2004). *Not just friends*. New York: Atria Books.

Gottman, J. M. (1999). *The marriage clinic*. New York: Norton.

Gottman, J. M., & Silver, N. (1999). *The seven principles for making marriage work*. New York: Crown.

Gottman, J. M., & DeClaire, J. (2001). *The relationship cure*. New York: Crown.

Gottman, J., Murray, J., Swanson, C., Tyson, R., & Swanson, K. (2002). *The mathematics of marriage: Dynamic nonlinear models*. Cambridge, MA: MIT Press.

Gottman, J. M., Gottman, J. S., & Declaire, J. (2006). *Ten lessons to transform your marriage: America's love lab experts share their strategies for strengthening your relationship*. New York: Crown.

Gottman, J. M., & Gottman, J. S. (2007). *And baby makes three: The six-step plan for preserving marital intimacy and rekindling romance after baby arrives.* New York: Crown.

Gottman, J. M. (2011). *The science of trust: Emotional attunement for couples.* New York: Norton.

Gottman, J., & Silver, N. (2012). *What makes love last? How to build trust and avoid betrayal.* New York: Simon & Schuster.

Jacobson, N., & Gottman, J. (1998). *When men batter women: New insights into ending abusive relationships.* New York: Simon & Schuster.

Kahneman, D. (2011). *Thinking, fast and slow.* New York: Farrar, Straus & Giroux.

Lederer, W. J. (1968). *The mirages of marriage.* New York: Norton.

Recommended Reading List

Books

Bergman, R. L. (2008). *Mindless psychoanalysis, selfless self psychology and further explorations*. Seattle, WA: The Alliance Press.

Dutton, D. (1995). *The domestic assault of women*. Seattle, WA: University of Washington Press.

Articles

Babcock, J. C., Gottman, J. M., Ryan, K. D., & Gottman, J. S. (2013). A component analysis of a brief psycho-educational couples' workshop: One-year follow-up results. *Journal of Family Therapy, 35*, 252–280. doi: 10.1111/1467-6427.12017

Babcock, J. C., Jacobson, N. S., Gottman, J. M., & Yerington, T. P. (2000). Attachment, emotional regulation, and the function of marital violence: Differences between secure, preoccupied, and dismissing violent and nonviolent husbands. *Journal of Family Violence, 15*(4), 391–409.

Babcock, J. C., Waltz, J., Jacobson, N. S., & Gottman, J. M.

(1993). Power and violence: The relation between communication patterns, power discrepancies, and domestic violence. *Journal of Consulting and Clinical Psychology, 61*(1), 40–50.

Berns, S. B., Jacobson, N. S., & Gottman, J. M. (1999) Demand-withdraw interaction in couples with a violent husband. *Journal of Consulting and Clinical Psychology, 67*(5), 666–674.

Bodenmann, G., Perrez, M., & Gottman, J. M. (1996). The significance of individual coping for a couple's interaction under stress. *Journal of Clinical Psychology,* 25 1–13 (in German).

Bradley, R. P. C., Friend, D. J., & Gottman, J. M. (2011). Supporting healthy relationships in low-income, violent couples: Reducing conflict and strengthening relationship skills and satisfaction. *Journal of Couple & Relationship Therapy, 10*(2), 97–116.

Buehlman, K., Gottman, J. M., & Katz, L. (1992). How a couple views their past predicts their future: Predicting divorce from an oral history interview. *Journal of Family Psychology,* 5(3–4), 295–318.

Carrere, S., Buehlman, K. T., Coan, J. A., Gottman, J. M., Coan, J. A., & Ruckstuhl, L. (2000). Predicting marital stability and divorce in newlywed couples. *Journal of Family Psychology,* 14(1), 42–58.

Carrere, S., & Gottman, J. M. (1999). Predicting divorce among newlyweds from the first three minutes of a marital conflict discussion. *Family Process,* 38(3), 293–301.

Carstensen, L. L., Gottman, J. M., & Levenson, R. W. (1995). Emotional behavior in long-term marriage. *Psychology & Aging, 10*(1), 140–149.

Carstensen, L. L., Graff, J., Levenson, R. W., & Gottman, J. M. (1996). Affect in intimate relationships: The developmental course of marriage. In C. Magai & S. McFadden (Eds.), *Handbook of emotion, adult developments, and aging* (pp. 227–247). San Diego, CA: Academic Press.

Coan, J., Gottman, J. M., Babcock, J., & Jacobson, N. S. (1997). Battering and the male rejection of influence from women. *Aggressive Behavior, 23*(5), 375–388. Wiley-Liss.

Driver, J. L. & Gottman, J. M. (2004a). Daily marital interations and positive affect during marital conflict among newlywed couples. *Family Process,* 43(3), 301–314.

Driver, J. L., & Gottman, J. M. (2004b). Turning toward versus turning away: A coding system of daily interactions. In P. K. Kerig & D. H. Baucom (Eds.), *Couple observational coding systems* (pp. 209–225). Mahwah, NJ: Erlbaum.

Driver, J., Tabares, A., Shapiro, A., Nahm, E. Y., & Gottman, J. (2003). Interactional patterns in marital success and failure: Gottman laboratory studies. In F. Walsh (Ed.), *Normal family process: Growing diversity and complexity* (3rd ed., pp. 493–513). New York: Guilford Press.

Finkel, E. J., & Rusbult, C. E., Kumashiro, M., & Hannon, P. A. (2002). Dealing with betrayal in close relationships: Does commitment promote forgiveness? *Journal of Personality and Social Psychology, 82,* 956-974.

Friend, D., Cleary Bradley, R., Thatcher, R., & Gottman, J. (2011). Typologies of intimate partner violence. *Journal of Family Violence.* doi: 10.1007/s10896-011-9392-2

Gortner, E., Berns, S., Jacobson, N. S., & Gottman, J. M. (1997). When women leave violent relationships: Dispelling clinical myths. *Psychotherapy: Theory, Research, Practice, Training,* 34(4), 343–352.

Gottman, J., Carrere, S., Swanson, C., & Coan, J. (2000). Reply to

"From basic research to interventions." *Journal of Marriage & the Family*, 62(1), 265–273.

Gottman, J., Driver, J., & Tabares, A. (2002). Building the Sound Marital House: An empirically-derived couple therapy. In A. S. Gurman & N. S. Jacobson (Eds.), *Clinical handbook of couple therapy* (3rd ed.). New York: Guilford Press.

Gottman, J., & Kimberly, R. (2005). The mismeasure of therapy: Treatment outcomes in marital therapy research. In W. M. Pinsof & J. L. Lebow (Eds.), *Family psychology: the art of the science* (pp. 65–89). New York: Oxford University Press.

Gottman, J., & Levenson, R. W. (2002). A two-factor model for predicting when a couple will divorce: Exploratory analyses using 14-year longitudinal data. *Family Process, 41*(1), 83–96.

Gottman, J., Levenson, R., &Woodin, E. (2001). Facial expressions during marital conflict. *Journal of Family Communication,* 1(1), 37–57.

Gottman, J., Ryan, K., Carrere, S., & Erley, A. (2002). Toward a scientifically based marital therapy. In H. Liddle, D. Santisteban, et al. (Eds.), *Family psychology: Science-based interventions* (pp. 147–174). Washington, DC: American Psychological Association.

Gottman, J., Ryan, K., Swanson, C., & Swanson, K. (2005). Proximal change experiments with couples: A methodology for empirically building a science of effective interventions for changing couples' interaction. *Journal of Family Communication,* 5(3), 163–190.

Gottman, J. M. (1998b). Psychology and the study of marital processes. *Annual Review of Psychology,* 49, 169–197.

Gottman, J. M. (1998c). Toward a process model of men in marriages and families. In A. Booth & N. Crouter (Eds.), *Men in families* (pp. 149–192). Hillsdale, NJ: Erlbaum.

Gottman, J. M. (1993b). The roles of conflict engagement, escalation or avoidance in marital interaction: A longitudinal view of five types of couples. *Journal of Consulting & Clinical Psychology, 61*(1), 6–15.

Gottman, J. M. (1993c). A theory of marital dissolution and stability. *Journal of Family Psychology, 7*(1), 57–75.

Gottman, J. M. (1995). Crime, hostility, wife battering, and the heart: On the Meehan et al. (2001) Failure to replicate the Gottman et al. (1995) typology. *Journal of Family Psychology, 15*(3), 409–414.

Gottman, J. M. (2001a). Meta-emotion, children's emotional intelligence, and buffering children from marital conflict. In C. Ryff & B. Singer (Eds.), *Emotion, social relationships and health,* Series in Affective Science (pp. 23–40).

Gottman, J. M. (2001b). What the study of relationships has to say about emotion research. *Social Science Information, 40*, 79–44.

Gottman, J. M., & Carrere, S. (1994). Why can't men and women get along? Developmental roots and marital inequities. In D. J. Canary & L. Stafford (Eds.), *Communication and relational maintenance* (pp. 203–229). San Diego, CA: Academic Press.

Gottman, J. M., Coan, J., Carrere, S., & Swanson, C. (1998). Predicting marital happiness and stability from newlywed interactions. *Journal of Marriage and the Family, 60*(1), 5–22.

Gottman, J. M., & Driver, J. L. (2005). Dysfunctional marital conflict and everyday marital interaction. *Journal of Divorce & Remarriage, 43*(3–4), 63–78.

Gottman, J. M., Driver, J., Yoshimoto, D., & Rushe, R. (2002). Approaches to the study of power in violent and nonviolent marriages, and in gay male and lesbian cohabiting relationships. In P. Noller & J. A. Feeney (Eds.), *Understanding marraige, developments in the study of couple interaction* (pp. 323–347). Cambridge: Cambridge University Press.

Gottman, J. M., & Gottman, J. S. (2008). Gottman method couple therapy. In A. S. Gurman (Ed.), *Clinical handbook of couple therapy* (pp. 138–166). New York: Guilford.

Gottman, J. M., & Katz, L. F. (2002). Children's emotional reactions to stressful parent-child interactions: The link between emotion regulation and vagal tone. *Journal of Marriage and Family Review,* 34(3/4), 265–283.

Gottman, J. M., Jacobson, N. S., Rushe, R. H., Shortt, J. W., Babcock, J., LaTaillade, J. J., & Waltz, J. (1995). The relationship between heart rate reactivity, emotionally aggressive behavior, and general violence in batterers. *Journal of Family Psychology,* 9(3), 227–248.

Gottman, J. M., & Levenson, R.W. (1992). Marital processes predictive of later dissolution: Behavior, physiology and health. *Journal of Personality and Social Psychology,* 63, 221–233.

Gottman, J. M., & Levenson, R.W. (1999a). What predicts change in marital interaction over time. *Family Process,* 38(2), 143–158.

Gottman, J. M., & Levenson, R.W. (1999b). How stable is marital interaction over time. *Family Process,* 38(2), 159–165.

Gottman, J. M., & Levenson, R. W. (2000a). Timing of divorce- predicting when a couple will divorce over a 14-year period. *Journal of Marriage and the Family,* 62, 737–745.

Gottman, J. M., & Levenson, R.W. (2000b). Dysfunctional marital conflict: Women are being unfairly blamed. *Journal of Divorce and Remarriage, 31*(3/4), 1–17.

Gottman, J. M., Levenson, R. W., Gross, J., Fredrickson, B., McCoy, K., Rosenthal, L., Ruel, A., & Yoshimoto, D. (2003). Correlates of gay and lesbian couples' relationship satisfaction and relationship dissolution. *Journal of Homosexuality, 45*(1), 23–43.

Gottman, J. M., Levenson, R. W., Swanson, C., Swanson, K., Tyson, R., & Yoshimoto, D. (2003). Observing gay, lesbian and heterosexual couples' relationships: Mathematical modeling of conflict interactions. *Journal of Homosexuality, 45*(1), 65–91.

Gottman, J. M., McCoy, K., Coan, J., & Collier, H. (1996). Vagal tone protects children from marital conflict. In J. M. Gottman (Ed.), *What predicts divorce: The measures*. Mahwah, NJ: Erlbaum.

Gottman, J. M., & Notarius, C. I. (2000). Decade review: Observing marital interaction. *Journal of Marriage & the Family, 62*(4), 927–947.

Gottman, J. M., & Notarius, C. I. (2002). Marital research in the 20th century and a research agenda for the 21st century. *Family Process, 41*(2), 159–197.

Hawkins, M., Carrere, S., & Gottman, J.M. (2002a). Marital sentiment override: Does it influence couples' perceptions. *Journal of Marriage & the Family, 64*(1), 193–201.

Hawkins, M., Carrere, S., & Gottman, J.M. (2002b). The marriage survival kit: A research-based marital therapy. *Journal of Marriage & the Family, 64*(1), 193–201.

Jacobson, N. S., Gottman, J. M., Gortner, E., Berns, S., & Shortt, J. W. (1998). The longitudinal course of battering: When do couples split up? When does the abuse decrease? *Violence and Victims, 11*(4), 371–378.

Jacobson, N. S., Gottman, J. M., Waltz, J., Rushe, R., et al. (1994). Affect, verbal content, and psychophysiology in the arguments of couples with a violent husband. *Journal of Consulting & Clinical Psychology,* 62(5), 982–988.

Jacobson, N. S., Gottman, J. M., Waltz, J., Rushe, R., Babcock, J., & Holtzworth-Monroe, A. (2000). Affect, verbal content, and psychophysiology in the arguments of couples with a violent husband. *Prevention & Treatment,* 3.

Jacobson, N. S., Gottman, J. M., & Shortt, J. W. (1995). The distinction between type 1 and type 2 batterers: Further considerations. *Journal of Family Psychology,* 9(3), 272–279.

Johnson, D. J., & Rusbult, C. E. (1989). Resisting temptation: Devaluation of alternative partners as a means of maintaining commitment in close relations. *Journal of Personality and Social Psychology,* 57, 967–980.

Levenson, R. W., Carstensen, L. L., & Gottman, J. M. (1994). Influence of age and gender on affect, physiology and their interrelations: A study of long-term marriages. *Journal of Personality and Social Psychology,* 67(1), 56–68.

Ryan, K. D., Carrere, S., & Gottman, J. M. (2000). Building a Sound Marital House. In M. K. White (Ed.), *Marriage in America*. Lanham, MD: Rowman & Littlefield.

Shapiro, A. F., & Gottman, J. (2005). Effects on marriage of a psycho-communicative-educational intervention with couples undergoing the transition to parenthood, evaluation at 1-year post-intervention. *Journal of Family Communication,* 5(1), 1-24.

Shapiro, A. F., Gottman, J. M., & Carrere, S. (2000). The baby and the marriage: Identifying factors that buffer against decline in marital satisfaction after the first baby arrives. *Journal of Family Psychology, 14*(1), 59–70.

Waltz, J., Babcock, J., Jacobson, N., & Gottman, J. M. (2000). Testing a typology of batterers. *Journal of Consulting & Clinical Psychology, 68*(4), 658–669.

Index

Note: Italicized page locators refer to figures.

Also available from

The Norton Series on Interpersonal Neurobiology

The Birth of Intersubjectivity: Psychodynamics, Neurobiology, and the Self
Massimo Ammaniti, Vittorio Gallese

Neurobiology for Clinical Social Work: Theory and Practice
Jeffrey S. Applegate, Janet R. Shapiro

Being a Brain-Wise Therapist: A Practical Guide to Interpersonal Neurobiology
Bonnie Badenoch

The Brain-Savvy Therapist's Workbook
Bonnie Badenoch

Neurobiologically Informed Trauma Therapy with Children and Adolescents: Understanding Mechanisms of Change
Linda Chapman

Intensive Psychotherapy for Persistent Dissociative Processes: The Fear of Feeling Real
Richard A. Chefetz

The Healthy Aging Brain: Sustaining Attachment, Attaining Wisdom
Louis Cozolino

The Neuroscience of Human Relationships: Attachment and the Developing Social Brain
Louis Cozolino

The Neuroscience of Psychotherapy: Healing the Social Brain
Louis Cozolino

From Axons to Identity: Neurological Explorations of the Nature of the Self
Todd E. Feinberg

Loving with the Brain in Mind: Neurobiology and Couple Therapy
Mona DeKoven Fishbane

Body Sense: The Science and Practice of Embodied Self-Awareness
Alan Fogel

The Healing Power of Emotion: Affective Neuroscience, Development & Clinical Practice
Diana Fosha, Daniel J. Siegel, Marion Solomon

Healing the Traumatized Self: Consciousness, Neuroscience, Treatment
Paul Frewen, Ruth Lanius

The Neuropsychology of the Unconscious: Integrating Brain and Mind in Psychotherapy
Efrat Ginot

The Impact of Attachment
Susan Hart

Art Therapy and the Neuroscience of Relationships, Creativity, and Resiliency: Skills and Practices
Noah Hass-Cohen and Joanna Clyde Findlay

Affect Regulation Theory: A Clinical Model
Daniel Hill

Brain-Based Parenting: The Neuroscience of Caregiving for Healthy Attachment
Daniel A. Hughes, Jonathan Baylin

Self-Agency in Psychotherapy: Attachment, Autonomy, and Intimacy
Jean Knox

Infant/Child Mental Health, Early Intervention, and Relationship-Based Therapies: A Neurorelational Framework for Interdisciplinary Practice
Connie Lillas, Janiece Turnbull

Clinical Intuition in Psychotherapy: The Neurobiology of Embodied Response
Terry Marks-Tarlow

Awakening Clinical Intuition: An Experiential Workbook for Psychotherapists
Terry Marks-Tarlow

A Dissociation Model of Borderline Personality Disorder
Russell Meares

Borderline Personality Disorder and the Conversational Model: A Clinician's Manual
Russell Meares

Neurobiology Essentials for Clinicians: What Every Therapist Needs to Know
Arlene Montgomery

Sensorimotor Psychotherapy: Interventions for Trauma and Attachment
Pat Ogden, Janina Fisher

Trauma and the Body: A Sensorimotor Approach to Psychotherapy
Pat Ogden, Kekuni Minton, Clare Pain

The Archaeology of Mind: Neuroevolutionary Origins of Human Emotions
Jaak Panksepp, Lucy Biven

The Polyvagal Theory: Neurophysiological Foundations of Emotions, Attachment, Communication, and Self-regulation
Stephen W. Porges

Affect Dysregulation and Disorders of the Self
Allan N. Schore

Affect Regulation and the Repair of the Self
Allan N. Schore

The Science of the Art of Psychotherapy
Allan N. Schore

The Mindful Brain: Reflection and Attunement in the Cultivation of Well-Being
Daniel J. Siegel

Pocket Guide to Interpersonal Neurobiology: An Integrative Handbook of the Mind
Daniel J. Siegel

Healing Moments in Psychotherapy
Daniel J. Siegel, Marion Solomon

Healing Trauma: Attachment, Mind, Body and Brain
Daniel J. Siegel, Marion Solomon

Love and War in Intimate Relationships: Connection, Disconnection, and Mutual Regulation in Couple Therapy
Marion Solomon, Stan Tatkin

The Present Moment in Psychotherapy and Everyday Life
Daniel N. Stern

The Neurobehavioral and Social-Emotional Development of Infants and Children
Ed Tronick

The Haunted Self: Structural Dissociation and the Treatment of Chronic Traumatization
Onno Van Der Hart, Ellert R. S. Nijenhuis, Kathy Steele

Changing Minds in Therapy: Emotion, Attachment, Trauma, and Neurobiology
Margaret Wilkinson

For complete book details, and to order online, please visit the Series webpage at wwnorton.com/Psych/IPNBseries